PEOPLE
MAKE
PROFITS

PEOPLE MAKE PROFITS

Keys to Corporate Survival in the '80s & '90s

Brian Spikes

BEAUFORT BOOKS, INC.
New York / *Toronto*

ISBN 0-8253-0084-3

Library of Congress Cataloging in Publication Data

Spikes, Brian.
   People make profits.

   Bibliography: p.
   1. Industrial management.   2. Personnel management.
I. Title.
HD31.S62   658   81-38460
ISBN 0-8253-0084-3 (pbk.)   AACR2

Published in the United States by Beaufort Books, Inc.
Published in Canada by General Publishing Co. Limited

First Edition

Table of Contents

I believe the real difference between success and failure in a corporation can very often be traced to the question of how well the organization brings out the great energies and talents of its people.

Thomas J. Watson Jr.
IBM Corporation

)

Preface

This book is not meant to be read as a text book in any way, shape, or form. It is not for students or teachers of *management* in the abstract. There are many excellent texts on management, and I am not suggesting they shouldn't be read. I know, however, that very few practicing managers have either the time or the inclination to read text books on management. This is very unfortunate, and must, in part, be attributed to the way such books are written.

I am quite aware that I have oversimplified a number of issues in my book, but I have done so with intent. I am a polemicist, not a text book writer. If you want to fine tune in the grey areas of management, read no further. This is not a book for you. I write to stimulate, provoke, and encourage thought and curiosity in managers who might otherwise shun books about their profession. It was Samuel Johnson, Englands greatest lexicographer, who once said, "Interest is the mother of attention, and attention is the mother of memory." I am trying to catch the interest and attention of managers and others, in the hope that they will be stimulated to seek further enlightenment about what has now become the world's fastest growing profession. In particular I recommend any or all of Peter Drucker's work. He is by far the most seminal thinker and writer on management.

Remember that the word *boss* is derived from the Dutch word *master*, as I pointed out in my earlier book, BOSS IS A FOUR LETTER WORD. Considering the importance of the managerial function in the 1980s, its abuse and misuse by Bosses is a national scandal. Canada is deathly short of managers who understand true leadership in the world of work.

I am quite aware for example, that no manager is one hundred percent Boss, or one hundred percent Leader. Every manager tends to lean in one direction or another, depending on the kind of person he or she is, and on the kinds of people and situations they are dealing with. There are many conflicting books on what constitutes effective leadership in the world of work, and they are all worth reading. My concern is to provide a rough-and-ready guide for those managers who are so often thrown into leadership positions with little or no preparation. This book may be helpful in providing them with a point of departure, rather than a point of arrival, in their thinking about their responsibilities.

If any Boss out there doubts that he is entering the twilight zone of management, he should take a quick glance at some of our more reputable business newspapers and journals. For example: "MANAGING NOW MEANS YOU CAN'T ACT LIKE A BOSS" — *Financial Post*. "WE NEED A REVOLUTION NOT AMONGST EMPLOYEES BUT AMONGST THE BOSSES" — *Royal Bank of*

Canada Newsletter. "HOW BOSSES CAN DRIVE THEIR EMPLOYEES MAD" — *Harvard Business Review*. Such headlines reflect the revolution that is going on in the world of work. The amount of knowledge in the world has been doubling about every ten years for the past 200 years. This means that by the time a child is ten years old, 50% of the world's knowledge has been developed before the child was born. The implication of this staggering increase of knowledge is that the goal of all learning is to keep on learning. There is no end. That is why professionals today in any field have to go back to school every year, not to get ahead, but just to stay where they are. Bosses who are not prepared to unlearn what was useful in the past will die on the job from a hardening of the categories, or an acute attack of super-shock. We live at a time when half the products on the market did not exist 15 years ago, when 90% of all the scientists who ever lived are alive to-day, and speed potential has in four decades increased from 400 mph to 18000 mph. The accelerating rate of change is increasing so rapidly that we cannot begin to imagine what developments will take place during the next ten or twenty years. If we were to guess, we would almost certainly be wrong. Herman Kahn reminds us that a study in 1937 missed predicting not only the computer, but atomic energy, antibiotics, radar, and jet propulsion.

The corporate dinosaurs currently lumbering across our managerial landscape are a deadly threat to our economic and social well being. They are, in fact, an endangered species. Witness their humiliation and defeat at the hands of more vigorous corporate bodies from other countries, particularly Japan.

CHAPTER I

The Deadly Disease of Corporate Dinosaurs

A corporate dinosaur is an organization that is operating under traditional management with little regard for the human needs of its employees, who in effect are reduced to the size of pygmies when compared with their potential for growth and contribution. They live dull, boring, and mentally impoverished lives on a day-to-day basis in the world of work. Pygmies are passionate complainers. Have you noticed? Complaints breed by the barrel full when they meet. Pygmies complain about everything except the true cause of their condition: unenlightened management.

The cortical mosaic in a corporation is the sum total of its conceptual resources. The cortical mosaic of the corporate dinosaur is comprised of traditional managers who think and behave like 19th century Bosses rather than 20th century Leaders. Remember, *Boss* is a four letter word that means, literally, "master." As Peter Drucker points out, there are no masters today — there are "only fellow-workers who are superior in rank, but equal in law." (*Management*, p. 241.)

Much is made of the need for energy conservation in our hard-pressed economy, but nothing is heard about the need to conserve, harness, and focus human energy into more productive channels. Have you ever stopped to think about the human energy that is wasted in Canada and the United States through needless conflict in labor-management disputes? Canada has the worst record in the world, with the possible exception of Italy. Think about it. Is that a record to be proud of? Hardly. And yet, where are the leaders in government and industry who are prepared to DO something about it? There are very few around. Here and there civil servants and academics are trying out experiments based on modern concepts, but they are pitifully few and inadequate when compared to the overwhelming need for change if we are to survive as an economically healthy nation.

When management and employees at all levels are united in pursuit of common goals in a spirit of mutual trust and support, morale and productivity will increase to the benefit of all. Leaders know that people feel their best when they are doing their best. In healthy corporations like IBM leaders at all levels spend more time developing and focussing human energy into productive channels than anything else. They must be doing something right, and, of course, they are. In the case of IBM they have been doing things right and doing the right things for more than forty years. That's why they are Number One.

However, the number of corporate dinosaurs lurching across the landscape is growing. It is nothing short of pathetic to witness these ailing monsters, now slurping in the public trough when once they were respected household names. How did they get into this desperate situation? They ignored the man in the street, the little people, the pygmies: employees and customers as well. Don't blame it all on Japanology, and say it can't be done in North America. It *can*. Japanese-managed companies in the US are outperforming American companies in the same industries. A Japanese-managed Sony plant in San Diego had 25% to 50% less turnover and absenteeism than other companies in the same industry in the same area. Some two hundred Japanese companies are operating in the United States with Japanese managers and American employees, and all of these companies are doing very well indeed.

Organizations that increase in size but not in wisdom are all set for internal ailments that eventually will bring them to their knees. The larger the organization the greater the danger that people will feel depersonalized, diminished, and depressed. Compared to their potential, employees will feel like pygmies because unenlightened managers (Bosses) do not know how to create a climate for growth.

Added to the factor of size is the problem of poorly defined purpose. When employees are not clear on the purpose of their efforts they lose interest and commitment to getting results. People cannot achieve what they cannot define. They get frustrated, withdraw, and shrink. Corporate dinosaurs guided by Bosses — like misguided missiles — unwittingly create systems that kill incentive, destroy morale, reduce productivity, and convert people into pygmies.

When more and more people do less and less,

everybody winds up doing very little. In 1979 a report on the Attorney General's Department revealed that 50,000 federal civil servants were working at jobs that required only 38,000 people. This unfailing tendency in corporate dinosaurs not unnaturally produces a loss of pride in employees, and eventually they retire 'on the job'.

Leaders of successful corporations know how to prevent *pygmyitis*. They have a passion for growth in people and profits. Leaders know that to improve productivity employees must be encouraged to stretch and grow so that they can do more tomorrow than they are doing today.

Here is what one successful Leader of a large Canadian enterprise has to say:

> By letting people become involved in solving a problem, in making decisions that affect them, they are more interested in their work and in the organization they work for. You get a better quality decision and a greater commitment from those who help make it.
>
> Struan Robertson —
> President and Chief Executive Officer
> Maritime Telegraph and Telephone Co.
> Halifax.

Sounds great, you say, but what about results? OK, here they are: Improved morale at Maritime Telegraph reduced absenteeism and turnover by 50%, and production has increased by almost 75% in the six months since the program was implemented.

CHAPTER II

Management by Witchcraft?

The psychological super-markets are booming; they never had it so good. Read the commercials in the glossy brochures from far-away places. Management Salvation is readily available . . . at a price you can't afford! Management by magic is all the rage. The current witches brew of ferment and fantasy is a product of management by desperation.

Itinerant practitioners of management witchcraft try to create the illusion that they don't know everything, and behave like private detectives with God on their side. Although they are vigorous in their condemnation of other witch doctors, they are quite willing to start their own witch hunting movements that spread like wild fire from one ailing corporate body to another. Nothing is more pitiable than to behold a corporate Boss standing amid the smouldering ruins of a snake-oil burnout, and the way he looks, you know he is searching for a cure for the cure.

The corporate twilight that precedes the death

of a dinosaur is haunted by a messianic belief in witchcraft. Consultants descend like vultures on the afflicted body, offering resurrection and a new life through corporate catharsis and confession. They remind me of decontamination squads offering to defuse highly explosive human resources.

A good witch doctor can always sell a spell. All he has to do is to offer to make Bosses more like Bosses, or pygmies more like pygmies, or both. Where Bosses run the show, he can't lose. Results, of course, are not guaranteed. Bosses actually do not know what to expect when they invest in training. They hope things will get better, that people will work harder, that productivity will increase. But, in the final analysis, they must trust the witch doctor. But *which* doctor? So many to chose from, so many tantalizing nostrums on the market.

Once the witch doctor is on board, a big pow-wow is held and the corporate community will be lulled — at least temporarily — into subservient tranquility. Bosses are outwardly awed, while the pygmies hold their breath and look for a trap. According to the magic-man, the crops will flourish, enemies will disappear, and everyone is promised everlasting life. The trouble is that all this magic seldom leads to any improvements in the corporate condition, and the CWD (corporate witch doctor) knows it. Of course he won't come right out and say so before the contract is signed. "To be or not to be, that is the question" for any CWD. He has to eat.

Mind you, this whole business is not quite as one sided as it sounds. It is not uncommon for a corporate Boss to use a CWD as a pawn on the corporate chess board. "We are following a consultants recommendations." That gets them off the hook, you see. Very convenient. Very well paid. Being a crafty bunch, they are seldom deceived, and they don't mind being paid to do someone else's dirty work.

A consultant, by the way, is not just a guy who borrows your watch to tell you the time, and then forgets to give you back your watch. The best definition of a consultant that I ever heard was given to me by Joe, my next door neighbor. His old tom cat used to crawl over my roof and wail on windy nights; one day, I complained mildly about this to Joe. He didn't say anything, but some months later I met him on the street. "Haven't heard your old tom for quite a while," I avowed. "Is he still around?" Joe nodded, "Yep, had him spayed a while back." "Oh really," I said, feeling slightly guilty for complaining, and wondering whether the old tom had me to blame for his deprivation. "Yep," continued Joe, "before I had him spayed he used to go out each night as a specialist. Now, he goes out as a consultant." I got the message.

I first discovered the full significance of Joe's remark shortly after I was invited to become a full-time, internal consultant with a very large government organization. I was given a nice office with a big desk and a magnificent view from a top floor of the Toronto Dominion Centre. After spending six weeks reading amendments to various legislative acts, I realized why many of my veteran colleagues were much immersed in calculating their pensions and pondering their retirement plans. There was nothing else to do. Oh, occasionally we were called upon to pacify the pygmies in the time honored way: paralysis through analysis. Promises, promises, and please . . . *please* the politicians. Keep your nose clean for the next twenty years and you'd be home free. No sweat. Just a slow death as a consultant, the way Joe had spelled it out. I wanted action and job satisfaction. I quit.

A corporate witch doctor will always be optimistic about his solutions, and he will often fuse problems and obfuscate issues. He is sure to have a solution for your problem, but it will probably be complicated and it will surely require incantations and numerous spells. Magical signs and symbols will be displayed on doors, desks, and walls. "THINK" was all the rage at one time. I wish I had a dollar for all the times I have encountered that maddening admonition. Unwittingly, Bosses reveal their unspoken assumptions about their employees with this kind of 'magic'. Obviously, pygmies don't think much, or at least, they are not interested in thinking about their work, so they must be told to THINK. One thing we have to admit about the CWD: he knows how Bosses think and he confirms what they want to hear. Bosses are full of wishful hearing.

A genuine, bona-fide, down-to-earth, honest-to-god consultant is hard to come by. For one thing, he has to be able to afford to be honest, and for another he has to have a rare combination of talent and empathy. Above all, he must be a creative listener in order to allow people to be themselves. He is not too interested in preaching or teaching *management* in the abstract. He is far more interested in helping people to solve the messy, day-to-day problems of management. In this way he may be able to create some islands of harmony in a mad ocean of strife and discontent. The truly effective consultant gets results by getting through to people as people . . . not pygmies. He knows that even the very best employees cannot achieve what they cannot define, and that success comes in *cans* and not *cannots*. He will strive mightily to convert problems into opportunities and opportunities into results.

The professional consultant who really knows what he is doing, is someone who understands that training people to do things right is only half the battle. The other half is training people to do the right things. In other words, efficiency, without effectiveness, is doomed to failure. His objective is to help managers to get results today, and to develop people for tomorrow.

Leaders never hire CWDs. They will hire results-oriented consultants who come clean at the start, and ask the vital question: "What results are you looking for, and how do you intend to measure them?" Then, and only then, can consultant and client forget about Analysis in Wonderland and get on with the job of setting behavioral objectives with relevant indicators to measure results.

CHAPTER III

Diagnosing the Dinosaur Condition

A management consultant — not a head hunter — is frequently called upon to take the temperature of the corporate body, diagnose its condition and then prescribe appropriate treatment. Unlike a medical doctor, however, a management consultant cannot bury his mistakes. He may wish that he could, but he can't. If he makes a mistake in diagnosis or prescription it can adversely affect the lives of thousands of people inside and outside the corporate body. How to be right when taking what must often be a rapid reading of organizational health is still more of an art than a science. To help me in the diagnostic phase of corporate consulting, I have developed a set of questions which I call verbal thermometers. I am very interested in the extent of dental decay in the corporate dinosaur because corporate caries are easily identified without any of the elaborate analysis or high power hokum beloved by behavioral hucksters. Long experience has taught me that corporations who have neglected their corporate teeth will not survive unless they undergo very extensive and very expensive dental surgery. When I carefully and gently explain this to corporate clients they shudder and often prefer to continue gumming their way to disaster than take corrective measures. The essence of dental hygiene is that prevention is better than cure. To ignore this conventional wisdom is to wake up one day with a raging toothache and realise too late that when important things are neglected over a period of time, they have a habit of becoming very urgent at a very inappropriate time. Corporate dinosaurs are no exception. So, you think I am putting you on, eh? Far from it. I am absolutely serious. OK, so what do I mean when I talk about corporate teeth and dental decay? And by the way, before I answer that question I want you to understand that I am not saying ALL corporations are dinosaurs or suffer from corporate decay. By no means. There are many corporate bodies that are very much alive and doing very well, thank you. They are in excellent health and show no signs of dental or any other kind of decay whatsoever. Why? Because they have no Bosses and no pygmies. Just lots of real live Leaders and lots of real live people who really love their work and are stretching and growing all the time.

The health of a corporate body, large or small, intimately affects its objectives and reasons for being. If the organization has lost sight of its purpose, it will probably redouble its efforts, start spinning its wheels and find that it's getting nowhere fast. If it has no objectives the corporate body is nothing more than a neck that grew up and haired over. Let's take a look at some of these so-called verbal thermometers because they will help to reveal the condition of a corporation's internal organs. You may apply these verbal thermometers to your own corporate body, if you wish. The answers may, or may not, reassure you, but they will certainly enlighten you.

VERBAL THERMOMETER #1

Why are you on the payroll?

"Ridiculous" you say. "Everybody knows why they're on a payroll!" Oh yea! You'd be surprised. From a healthy corporation's point of view the only reason why anyone is on a payroll, whether it be in the public, private, or voluntary sector, and don't forget I am including in these categories any organization that is incorporated by law, is to make a very specific contribution to the objectives of the organization. Ah, now you can see why I mentioned objectives in the preceding paragraph. If there are no objectives, or if they are poorly defined, or if only a few people know what they are, you have the first and most important symptom of pygmyitis. If a bunch of guys go out hunting but have no idea what they are hunting, they are not likely to get very good results.

Right? . . . Right!

It often falls to my lot to insert verbal thermometer #1 into the cortical mosaic of quite senior managers who inhabit a wide range of corporate entities. These managers — they are always Bosses — find it very difficult to answer my question. They may say things like: "Well, I'm on the payroll because I have 600 men reporting to me." Or, "I'm on the payroll because I'm in charge of data processing." Then I have to explain, as gently as possible, that their replies describe only the position of authority they hold. They say nothing about the specific contributions they should be making to the objectives of the organization. A Leader in a healthy corporate body would answer such a question along these lines: "I'm on the payroll to get the following results," and then he will proceed to spell them out. See what I mean? Good. We are both making progress.

When managers are not crystal clear on why they are on a payroll I immediately suspect poor health in the corporate head in terms of poorly defined objectives. Without objectives a corporation has no 'get-up-and-go'. Such a condition can only exist under Bosses, and it guarantees the existence of pygmies. Why? Because if the Boss is not clear on results expected, neither are his employees.

Consequently the Boss will be overwhelmed with pygmies, coming at him from all directions, asking what to do and probably how to do it. Leaders don't have this problem because they have set out well-defined objectives, and communicated these with clarity to everyone at every level. All employees have a good grip on the purpose and priorities of the organization at all times.

VERBAL THERMOMETER #2

What is your most important responsibility as a manager?

Every manager has many responsibilities. We all know that. But the fact is that some responsibilities are more important than others, and one in particular is more important than all the rest. Does that sound like too much? Well if it does, I suspect that you are a Boss rather than a Leader.

Why? Well, think about it carefully. You don't believe me? Let me tell you something, and when I have told you, go and check it out with some independent source that is truly knowledgeable in this field. If you don't know what your most important responsibility is, and if you are not spending at least 25% of your time on it, I have news for you: you are a Boss and every son-of-a-gun working for you is a pygmy! Still puzzled? The single most important responsibility of any manager is to train and develop his or her people to the highest and most excellent standard of performance so that they do their job and do it willingly. If you don't demand high standards from your people, they will not stretch and grow, and you will never be able to delegate responsibilities to them.

VERBAL THERMOMETER #3

How do you know when you have done a good job?

If the corporation is a dinosaur the answer will be something to the effect that "If I don't hear anything from my Boss, I assume I'm doing a good job." If you are a manager and think this is a good answer — Good Night! Across this fair land of ours, about the only time a pygmy will find out whether he is doing a good job or not is when he is being fired. Then — to the amazement of the pygmy — his Boss starts telling him things he never knew before. Like what he really should have been doing for the last twelve months or more. When the pygmy tries to explain that he was never told what results were required, the Boss gets madder than hell, and chews him up. Pygmies can't win. They are never right. Only the Boss is right. Every time, all the time. No wonder so many corporate dinosaurs are getting about 20% of their employees' true capacity . . . if they are lucky.

VERBAL THERMOMETER #4

What is the we-they ratio in your department?

I explain to the manager that a consultant can tell a great deal about organizational health if he can find out roughly how many times employees talk about *they* as opposed to *we*. For example: "Why can't *they* find out for *themselves*," or, "If I go and ask *them, they* don't know until someone tells *them*," or, "The engineers didn't know about this, but when I tried to tell *them, they* said, '*You're* not an engineer,'" or, "If *they* would only explain their new schedule *we* would have fewer problems around here," or, "Even if *we* come up with a good idea, *they* give us no recognition."

When more people are talking about *they* than *we*, it means they do not feel they belong. They are not on the team as partners, with a stake in the enterprise. They are just another bunch of pygmies griping in the gut of the dinosaur, slowing down its reflexes, and contributing to cortical confusion in the corporate cranium.

The dinosaurs of antiquity that roamed our continent were the largest, strongest, and best organized creatures of their time. We know what happened to them. When their environment changed, they were unable to meet the challenge of change. Remember, dinosaurs had a very small head to control a very large body as well as a variety of anatomical extremities. The corporate dinosaurs of today have a very small head in terms of Bosses at the top who call the shots and make decisions for others to follow. They also have a number of anatomical extremities in the shape of far flung departments, branches, divisions, etc., which they are finding increasingly difficult to manage.

The lesson is clear: if the corporate dinosaur wants to survive it must adapt to change and learn to decentralize its cortical function throughout its anatomical extremities. In other words, delegate by results required to the lowest possible level of decision-making. When done effectively, this is the surest guarantee that people won't become pygmies. With increased responsibility they will stretch and grow.

VERBAL THERMOMETER #5

How are things going in your department?

The answer to this seemingly innocuous question can be very disturbing, but very revealing. I remember a Boss responding with these words: "Oh things seem to be going quite smoothly, I guess." Then he paused, and then a slight glaze appeared over his eyes as he continued: "But, you know something, there is just one thing . . . sometimes I get the feeling that I don't seem to have as much control over what is going on around here as I used to have."

This is the first symptom of Super-Shock. It was too late for the Boss I am referring to. I remember shaking the damp, trembling hand of frustration as he offered to show me around the plant. It soon became apparant that I was talking to the Boss of a corporate body that was sinking slowly into extinction.

Corporate dinosaurs are highly vulnerable to Boss-Shock because over the years many of their managers have developed a hardening of the categories. What they look at is not what they see, it is what they believe.

Now that you have some idea of what I am writing about, perhaps you will have the courage to accompany me as I travel further into the realm of description and prescription for corporate survival in the world of work.

CHAPTER IV

From Pygmies to People

Some of our problems are our own fault. We lost contact with our own employees. Managements in large companies say that they get too big to stay in personal contact with their employees. We swallowed that. Now, however, I think that the opposite is true. The larger we get, the more important it is for us to emphasize personal contact by top management down through all levels. We've been doing it all wrong. We stumbled over our own assumptions.

(a quote from a CEO mentioned by Professor L. B. Barnes, in "Managing The Paradox of Trust," *Harvard Business Review*, March 81)

Unspoken assumptions, implicit in the structure of language, are blind spots that cause Bosses to be counter-productive in much of their behavior. Linguistic polarities and dichotomies which diminish are abundant in the everyday vernacular of Bosses — "Good and bad employees" — "We have to tell them what to do" — "Don't waste time explaining to them" — "They are paid to work, we are paid to think" — are a few common examples of the way in which language can be counter-productive.

A method for turning pygmies into people has been around for more than forty years under the title: Work Simplification. Nothing new, but it's creating new miracles. (See, *Factory*, Sept. 1965, "Mogy's Work Simplification System is creating new miracles," by Auren Uris)

Back in the 1930s, Allan H. Mogenson was appalled at the waste of human resources and the misdirection of human energy. He realized that people don't resist change, but they do resist being changed. Mogy developed and conducted a unique training course over a period of forty years. The process has been adopted and adapted by Leaders in business and industry under different titles. Strictly speaking, it is a form of job enrichment, but it is also known as a Work-Improvement or Team-Improvement program. The rationale for his work simplification program (WSP) is simply that employees lack skills that would enable them to formulate work improvements. WSP is a down-to-earth process that is easy for any work group to apply and manage themselves in a job improvement program.

WSP's are related to quality control circles which are widespread in Japan and are now beginning to catch on in North America. The Japanese were introduced to quality control methods by Dr. W. Edward Deming of the United States after W.W. II to help Japanese industry back on its feet.

Today, Dr. Deming is a national hero in Japan and each year a Deming Award is presented to the Japanese company with the most outstanding achievement in quality control.

It is interesting to speculate why WSP's and QCC's never really caught on in North America. No management method is a prophet in its own country. But American management methods, coupled with the ferocious motivation of a work force determined to win the peace after losing the war, has made the West — and particularly North Americans — realize what can be achieved by workers who are encouraged to manage themselves.

Japanese success was made in the United States. Reason? The Japanese are practicing 100 percent what Mogensen and Deming were preaching in the United States fifty years ago!

Allan Mogenson, who is still going strong at 77, believes that every employee gets satisfaction out of improving his work, and that every employee has the ability to improve his job. All that employees need is a method to use, under a supervisor who is not a Boss but a Leader, in the sense of being an advisor or consultant. This approach coincides with Peter Drucker's belief that the most important responsibility is to educate people to manage themselves. A Work Simplification Program involves five steps:

1) The employees select a job they want to improve
2) The employees gather all the available facts about the job
3) They 'brain storm' every detail of the job
4) They select the best possible method to improve the job

5) They install the method and monitor the results.

This method works because it can provide employees with psychological and financial benefits not possible under Bosses.

Remember this: Most employees want to achieve, but just giving them the opportunity is not enough. At Zeiss, IBM, and in Japan, engineers do not organize the work of employees. It is assumed that when workers understand work, they will organize a way in which to do it. Peter Drucker, that most prestigious practitioner of corporate correction, has clearly distinguished between making work productive and workers achieving. Work, he says, has a logic all its own. Working has none. In other words it's fine for engineers to organize work according to the logic of work, but it's not right to organize working according to the same logic. Drucker emphasizes a point that seems to be lost on Bosses and obvious to Leaders: "Work belongs to the world of things, whereas working belongs to the world of people. "Work," says Drucker, "is not unskilled or skilled, it is the worker who is skilled or unskilled." (*Management*, p. 198.)

Continuous training for self-improvement is a major factor in developing super-vision. The employee develops a wider vision of the whole work operation in which he is involved. The focus is on organizing responsibility for the job. To this end, Vitamin I (Information) is the critical ingredient in the daily diet of work. Deprive employees of Vitamin I and I will guarantee that you will create a permanent lack of loyalty in your organization. Here is the formula:

1) Give no information
2) Implement change without notice
3) Make decisions without consultation

That's it. It works . . . with a vengeance.

The optimum climate for conducting Work Simplification Programs is one in which adult — adult, I am OK, you are OK — attitudes predominate. The leader of a WSP group can greatly reduce his parent-child posture by getting volunteers involved in recording the ideas of the group. An idea that will involve other groups laterally, above, or below, must be submitted to representatives of those groups for discussion and approval. If such ideas are not approved, it is imperative that reasons are passed on to the group originating the suggestion.

Down through the ages men have used the natural hunting or work group as a ready-made means to solve problems. In any corporate body, such groups will occur naturally at any level. It makes sense, therefore, to capitalize on such groups, and to deal with any problems that relate to its functions, whether they be product improvement, quantity, or cost.

Management by perception is something that should be emphasized more in management education, because by changing an employee's perception an employee will often change his behavior, without having to be 'motivated'. He must see the problem from management's point of view, and appreciate the mutual benefit to be gained from acting accordingly.

A variation of WSP is Team Problem Solving in which the leader of a work group draws three columns on a flip chart or on a blackboard as follows:

LIST	LIST	LIST
PROBLEMS	SOLUTIONS	5 W's
		(who, what, when, where and why)

The work group will identify some of the current problems that they feel are important and list them in the first column. They select the most urgent problem, and then define it carefully. At this point you would do well to remember that the biggest problem in solving any problem is the problem of stating the problem. (see also, Chapter VIII, "The Yen For Zen.") Old John Dewey said it more succinctly: "A problem well defined is a problem half solved".

The next step is to brain-storm for possible solutions. It is surprising how few people in management have used the brain-storming technique, which has been around for a long time. It is not just a matter of getting a few people together and then asking for ideas. A very specific technique should be used to generate volume of ideas, and then refine, sift, and screen these ideas in light of some very specific and relevant criteria.

I have used brain-storming techniques in a wide range of problem-solving situations for organizations as varied as hospitals, children's aid societies, manufacturing plants, and paper-making companies.

The essential thing to do is to prove to each group before brain-storming that the technique works, and, if followed, will be highly productive in terms of ideas. To do this, I instruct the group to prepare for a time test as follows: "OK, you have three minutes. I want you to write down as many good ideas that you can think of for using an ordinary paper-clip." After three minutes the group counts up the number of ideas each member has generated and puts them on one side.

If the group is fairly large, say twenty to twenty-five people, I may say, "I want you to break into groups of five and imagine you are a special committee and you have been asked to brain-storm for all the good ideas you can think up that would attract visitors to North America in the coming year." I usually give the groups about fifteen minutes to complete the task. While they are having fun with this project — they always do — I listen carefully to the comments from individual members. Fascinating. Why? Because I want to record and feed back all manner of negative thinking expressed and implied by the unspoken assumptions implicit in the words of the group members. For example: "That wouldn't work" — "That is too far out" — "That would cost too much money" — and so on. When the fifteen minutes is up I point out to the group that they have been striving for GOOD ideas and subjecting their ideas to all sorts of restrictive criteria based on conventional thinking. This may or may not impress the group, but it will not convince them of anything in particular until you ask them to brain-storm again, this time without criticism of any idea, and listing ALL THE IDEAS, regardless of whether anyone thinks they are good or bad.

A three minute exercise will suffice using some relatively mundane object, such as a pencil, a man's belt, or something similar. When each member counts up the total of his ideas, he or she will discover on an average that they have produced three to four times the number of ideas they thought up the first time around. Of course, not all of these ideas are going to be the greatest thing since sliced bread. BUT, with a larger numerical base to work from, the chances of finding the nuggets of gold are much greater.

This is such a simple technique, and rewarding in so many ways that I am emphasizing its use, specifically for people preservation, in any corporate body at any level.

The third and final step in the brain-storming process is to apply a feasibility criterion to the most likely ideas, and then prepare them for implementation. If you want read up the full dope on this cracking good technique, and remember, it is only a technique, get hold of Alex Osborne's, *Applied Imagination* (1953). It will be worth the effort. If you become really interested in following up, you can attend one of the summer workshops on Creative Problem Solving run by Dr. J. Parnes, Director of the Faculty of Creative Education at Buffalo State University, New York.

CHAPTER V

Semantic Sanitation

Bosses are victims of verbal voodoo because they don't know which words are witch words, and they wind up bewitched, bothered, and bewildered. Caught in the polarities of two-valued logic, they communicate with 'subordinates' in terms of either/or: something or someone is right or wrong; good or bad; for or against. There are no grey areas for compromise because Bosses are tuned into black or white pictures of the world they live in.

Leaders involve their people in team problem solving sessions because their psychic antennae are searching for subtleties that lie between the extremes of either/or. They avoid the verbal treadmills that produce semantic malnutrition because they are aware of the influence of language on human behavior. It is generally agreed that about 80% of a manager's time is spent in communications: reading, writing, speaking, and listening, and yet, I have never seen a book on management that deals with the importance of semantics.

Keep in mind that properly understood

semantics goes beyond the meanings of words; in a general sense, it deals with the influence of language on human behavior. Semantics is very much concerned with creating 'awareness', that word again, of unspoken assumptions implicit in the structure of language which unconsciously influence the way we respond to people and things. Bosses scream about 'bad communication', but remain unaware of their responsibilities in this regard. I know Bosses who have become light headed from overindulgence in high level abstractions found in traditional texts of 'Management' and 'Communications'. Even more incredible is that very few Bosses are aware of the purpose of communication in management. Over the past ten years I have asked hundreds of managers to define the meaning of communication in management. In groups of five or six I let them struggle until they get tired and then ask them for their definition. Over and over they will talk about the importance of sending and receiving messages, getting people to understand and so on, but the most critical purpose of communication is not mentioned.

There are two critical ingredients in any meaningful definition of communication. One is UNDERSTANDING, and the second is RESULTS. Leaders communicate to get results; they communicate to change behavior so that results will be obtained. You would think this is obvious, wouldn't you? Well, to Bosses it isn't. It makes me wonder what has happened to management education. If Bosses are not acutely aware of the purpose of communication, and more than 80% of their time is spent in communicating, is it any wonder that things get screwed up?

A Leader knows perfectly well that communication in management is results oriented. Bosses know what isn't so. Bosses get into all kinds of trouble with their people because they jump to conclusions based on inference rather than fact. One Boss fired a girl in a typing pool because she did not answer when he called her several times. The battery in her hearing aid was dead. His unspoken semantic assumption about her behavior was that she was insubordinate. Another Boss rushed into a warehouse one night and fired a man slumped over a telephone at a desk. He was fast asleep. Turned out the guy was a salesman from another company checking with his home office on a late delivery. A Leader slows down semantically in this kind of situation, and puts the brakes on before he jumps to conclusions about human behavior. He will check carefully before acting rashly.

People who become pygmies under Bosses are constantly subjected to linguistic lacerations. They are bombarded with notices, memos, ultimatums, orders and instructions on everything from pot to policies. When the pygmies get fed up with all this semantic impurity they occasionally revolt. I discovered an interesting example of this in the washroom of a very large public utility. Stuck on the wall was the following communication:

TO ALL PERSONNEL:

As a result of automation, as well as a declining work load, management must of necessity take steps to reduce our work force. A reduction-in-staff plan has been developed which appears to be the most equitable at the present time.

Under the plan, older employees will be placed on early retirement, thus permitting the retention of those employees who represent the future of the company.

Therefore, a program to phase out older personnel by the end of the current fiscal year via early retirement will be placed into effect immediately. The program shall be known as RAPE (Retire Aged Personnel Early).

Employees who are RAPE'd will be given the opportunity to seek other jobs within the company, provided that while they are being RAPE'd they request a review of their employment status before actual retirement takes place. This phase of the operation is called SCREW (Survey of Capabilities of Retired Early Workers).

All employees who have been RAPE'd and SCREW'd may then apply for a final review. This will be called SHAFT (Study by Higher Authority Following Termination).

Program policy dictates that employees may be RAPE'd once and SCREW'd twice, but they may get the SHAFT as many times as their Boss deems appropriate.

This notice was the subject of much conversation and amusement among the pygmies because it appeared shortly after the Bosses had made a number of decisions affecting all employees, without any consultation whatsoever. Each Boss received a copy of the notice and it was widely distributed throughout the utility.

When washrooms become the medium for communication with Bosses, then, as Marshall C. McLuhan said, "the medium is the message."

John Galbraith once said, "Corporate life is like marriage without sex." It's dead because there is no meaningful communication.

Dr. S. I. Hayakawa, world famous semanticist, explains in one of his best selling books, *Language In Thought and Action*, that people look at life through a pair of linguistic spectacles fixed by the culture into which they are born, including its language. He demonstrates the importance of being able to communicate at different levels of abstraction in order to avoid being stuck in cloud cuckoo land. Relating words to words is a well known disease that afflicts a number of very highly educated Bosses, and they are very good at it. It may read well in the annual report but it fails to communicate with the employees, because they don't speak that language. A Leader will relate words to things when he is dealing with the troops. He doesn't go over their heads with abstractions. Example: what is your definition of *morale*? If you are a high level abstractor and semantically impure, you will find nothing wrong with this phrase: "Morale is something to do with how employees feel." I would rather hear you say something like this: "Good morale must be measured by specific indicators in terms of absenteeism, down-time, turnover, complaints, productivity, accidents, punctuality, innovation, and new ideas." These indicators will give you a better reading of morale because they help you to relate words to things that can be measured. Operational definitions enable one to climb down the ladder of abstraction and be very specific about what we mean.

The old conundrum that tormented the ancients was: "How many angels can dance on the head of a pin?" They couldn't come up with an answer, but *we* can by using an operational approach: "Bring me some angels and a pin and we'll find out!"

Questions can be more important than answers, if you know how to use them. Bosses don't. Socrates did. When asked how he happened to discover relativity, Einstein replied, "By challenging an axiom."

An effective Leader is prepared to discuss a question without settling it, rather than settling it without discussing it. A Japanese manager asks three times as many questions as he gives answers. He knows he does not know everything and he knows that an important criterion for an effective manager will lie in what his employees remember after they have forgotten what he said. In an age of increasing conformity, what healthy corporate bodies need is not more and more Bosses to spew out instant answers. They need more and more employees at all levels who are able and willing to question and requestion their assumptions about the work they do. Assumptions about people who work for us will determine our attitudes toward them in the office, in the plant, in the cafeteria, and the washroom.

Verbal hygiene and semantic sanitation are basic requirements for a healthy mind, but most Bosses' attitudes toward their responsibility in this regard reminds me of the keeper at the zoo who was asked whether a hippo was male or female. He replied: "That would be of interest only to another hippo."

How to survive verbal warfare in a semantic no-man's land is an essential prerequisite for an effective Leader in the world of work. I recommend *Language In Thought and Action* for your managerial survival kit. You won't find it mentioned in any management curriculum that I know of — for the simple reason that most management books are written by people who think running a business is the same as running a zoo.

Try a cortical tango with the idea that knowledge may be power, but effective knowledge is that which includes knowledge of one's knowledge. In other words, if you want to be a Leader, you need to know not only what you know, but also how you know what you know. "Know thyself" is the ultimate wisdom. In semantics, this translates into: "Know thy language," and become aware of its unspoken assumptions. It will reduce tension, clarify issues, and save time.

CHAPTER VI

Why War in the World of Work?

The war between management and labor has evolved from master-servant relationships down through the centuries. The difference between masters and servants used to be measured in terms of money and knowledge. No more. With the advent of unions, mass education, and television, the discernible criteria of master-servant relationships has virtually disappeared. Less than one hundred years ago most workers were illiterate. Today, most workers have had at least twelve years of schooling. Opportunities for continuing education are almost boundless, thanks to public libraries, evening and correspondence courses, and television. Take a look at any parking lot outside any office or factory building today. Can you tell the difference between the cars of the masters and the servants?

In our increasingly homogenized society, masters and servants watch the same TV programs, eat the same kinds of food, drive the same kinds of cars, and live in similar type homes.

Although the gap between masters and servants has closed dramatically in terms of education and income, it's still wide apart in the world of work. Dictatorship still remains supreme at the workplace for most employees, and unions maintain an adversarial stance to further the interests of their members.

The time is more than ripe to move from adversarial to collaborative relationships if corporate dinosaurs want to survive the impact of change in the 1980s. Curious isn't it. Bosses, who will fight to defend democracy as a political institution, will fight to prevent democracy in the world of work. Why? Because they feel threatened with a loss of power. They think they will no longer be able to *manage* their pygmies. They are afraid that their pygmies might want to become people. The all important question that must be raised is this: Can a nation afford to let backward Bosses stand in the way of economic survival. The answer, of course, is a resounding NO. Democracy in the workplace is not incompatible with the principles of free enterprise, but Bosses must recognize that it takes enlightened leadership to manage people in a democratic fashion. Is that too much to expect in a nation that proudly proclaims its democratic institutions?

Countries with the least number of industrial disputes are Sweden and West Germany. They are both highly unionized and practice democracy as a way of life. Canada and the United States have the greatest number of disputes and do not practice democracy. The 'Doctors of Industrial Salvation' in Canada are loud in their preachments against industrial democracy. "It won't work in Canada," they wail, "We have a different tradition." They keep saying this about the Japanese, but the

Japanese are not listening. They are laughing all the way to the bank. Japanese management in USA and Canada is here, and it is here to stay, in spite of our 'Doctors of Industrial Relations'. Why don't they get their heads out of the sand? Answer: They get too well paid for telling Bosses what Bosses want to hear.

Not too long ago, one of these 'Archangels of Academe' told an enthusiastic audience of Bosses that it is in the best interests of workers to work harder now that unemployment is higher. If he is prepared to preach this nonsense to the public, what in God's name is he preaching to his students . . . at public expense, in more ways than one. He is still perpetuating the old 19th century myth that employees should work harder instead of working smarter. How many corporate Bosses have been crippled by this incredible crap during their 'management education'? War in the world of work is perpetuated very largely by the myths of management and unions working against each other.

It is too much to expect that either management or unions will ever declare unconditional surrender to the other side. However, it is more than possible that under enlightened leadership they could get together in a spirit of understanding, collaboration, and team work, and start to WORK TOGETHER in pursuit of a common goal: SURVIVAL.

John Dewey once declared that a moral equivalent of war must be found, if the human species is to survive. In this regard it must be said that the race for space is fulfilling a noble mission. In the world of work, the moral equivalent to war must be found in the challenge to preserve the dignity and values of man. Production is not an end in itself. Production is for people, and each person needs to find some ultimate value, some ultimate meaning in the experience we call work, because work is a part of life, and life without meaning is a form of death.

CHAPTER VII

Memo to the Personnel Boss

Although it is obvious that people acquire useful skills and knowledge, it is not obvious that these skills and knowledge are a form of capital, that this capital is a part of a definite investment that has grown in Western Societies at a faster rate than conventional (nonhuman) capital, and that its growth may well be the most distinctive feature of the economic system.

Theodore Schultz — Nobel Prize winner in Economics 1979. Presidential address to the American Economic Association.

Bosses have yet to grasp the meaning in the message delivered by Schultz. They have failed to recognize the significance of human resources accounting, and return on investment in human resources. Unfortunately, they are aided and abetted by person-

nel Bosses who are ignorant or indifferent to growing people. There are Bosses in personnel positions
who would rather be *do-gooders* and than *good-
doers*. These guys are members of the happy,
happy school of human relations. Smile, pat the
pygmies on their heads, and all will be well. Wake-
up! Management by perception should be your
forte. You may not be able to change top management's behavior, but if you know how to change
their perception they will change their behavior
toward you and your programs for leadership.
Every personnel manager worth his salt should be
promoted immediately and made a vice-president
of Human Energy. Are you worth your salt? Never
mind your salary. If you can get results . . . your
salary will take care of itself. Try this quiz before we
go any further:

1) Can you read your company's financial
   statement?
2) Do you know the profit level of your company?
3) Do you know the long range plans of your
   company?
4) Do you know the differences between a
   statement of good intentions and a statement of objectives?
5) Is your management succession chart up to
   date?
6) Have you developed a manpower development plan?
7) Do you know the difference between training and development?
8) Do you know how your department makes
   money for the company?

If you have trouble answering these questions, I have news for you. *You* are a personnel Boss, not a personnel Leader. How can you expect to have credibility with top management if you have not done your homework? A personnel Leader is aiming for return on investment in human capital, and what's more, he knows how to get it. Do you? If you don't know . . . you won't grow. That's not a threat. That's a promise. You see, your job is to convert corporate dinosaurs into corporate communities capable of increasing productivity and enhancing the quality of working life for every single employee. No exceptions!

You must lead in the battle of hearts vs heads, and you must build the bridge from confrontation to co-operation. This is not wishful thinking. For you, it is enlightened self-interest.

Remember, you are the pathfinder in quest of COMMUNITY. WHAT HAVE YOU DONE FOR YOUR COMMUNITY IN THE LAST 24 HOURS?

CHAPTER VIII

The Yen For Zen

As corporate dinosaurs reel under the impact of Japanese imports, thoughtful managers are slowly developing a yen for Zen. Why? Because they yearn to understand what it is that enables Japanese industry to be so highly efficient and effective.

The key to understanding the Japanese management phenomena may lie in a principle of Zen, not widely known in the Western world. The word Zen means, "wake up," and originated in the awakening of an Indian prince named Guatama, whose teachings spread to Japan and many other parts of Asia. A Zen Master teaches his pupils — among other things — to "wake-up" and generate psychic energy to deal with unresolved problems and dilemmas.

One of the biggest problems in converting Bosses into Leaders — and believe it or not, this can be done — is to help them to develop their A.Q. (Awareness Quotient) rather than their I.Q. I have said it before, and I will say it again, Bosses are not stupid; they are often very intelligent and very hard working. Unfortunately, in the 1980s these desirable characteristics are not sufficient to ensure survival. Awareness is sometimes more important than intelligence, because without awareness, intelligence and energy are simply misdirected, wasted, and squandered. Perceptive observers are aware that this problem is just one more aspect of the 'human energy crisis'.

Corporate dinosaurs are full of Bosses who are quite unaware that they could achieve a quantum leap in performance and productivity if they would stop treating their people like pygmies and start treating them as persons. Does that sound reasonable? "Yes," you may reply . . . "in theory, but how does it work in practice?" That is a fair question and I will try to answer it.

Let us take a look at how it is done in Japan. In that country management decisions are reached by consensus. In a Japanese company, a proposed decision will be discussed thoroughly at all levels until agreement is achieved on all aspects of the problem. Then, and only then, is a decision made.

In the West, when a matter arises that requires a decision, managers look for answers to questions — whereas Japanese managers spend a great deal of time defining questions. For the Japanese, the critical importance of defining the question is to determine the need for a decision. This is in line with the old saying that a problem well defined is a problem half solved. The Japanese pursue this principle in decision-making with untiring tenacity.

When consensus is achieved in a Japanese company it means that they have agreed on the need to make a decision. Up to that point, there is no attempt to come up with possible answers or solutions, so that participants are not prematurely forced into a partisan position either for or against. They thoroughly define the problem before they attempt to create a solution.

Western companies who order products from Japan have observed that a Japanese company will send over groups of their representatives in several waves to learn at first hand the exact needs of the potential customer. The reason for this initially puzzling behavior to Western companies lies in the Japanese policy of making sure that employees from all departments of a company will obtain a clear understanding of customer requirements at first hand. When everyone is clear on the nature of a customer's needs and problems, then the Japanese make decisions in a hurry. This practice often confounds Western companies, long accustomed to hot footing their sales force to "get orders" by hook or by crook . . . get them "fast," and then spend weeks and sometimes months trying to sort out what the customer really meant when he specified requirements. Result? Unbelievable screw-ups, delays, and endless frustration for all involved.

When a Japanese company finally accepts an order, everyone who will be involved understands clearly what is required and when it is required. They deliver on schedule. There are no excuses.

Some time ago, Herman Kahn predicted that, by the year 2000 AD, Japan will be the leading industrial super-power in the world. He explained that one reason for their success may lie in the fact that junior employees are first involved in defining a problem, and then their ideas are submitted to a higher level of management that must discuss them thoroughly, and then pass on their recommendations to top management for a final decision. Kahn points out that the participation of all employees in this fashion not only gives all concerned what I refer to as Vitamin O (Opportunity) and Vitamin Rl (Responsibility) in their daily diet of work, it also greatly strengthens employee morale throughout the whole company.

If you stop to reflect on some of the problems experienced at General Motors, Ford, Chrylser, and others, it may make you wonder why some of these corporations don't hire a few Japanese managers to teach them how to lead, not just manage. After all, the Japanese have learned a great deal from the Western world during the last 100 years. Are we too proud to learn from them? The fact is that a number of companies in the West are seriously considering Japanese methods to improve performance and productivity, and a few have already achieved outstanding results. Quality control groups of workers are widely established throughout Japanese industry, and they practice something known as *Jishu Kanri*, or "voluntary management." Small groups of workers meet several times weekly to solve everyday problems; their success has been amazing. They meet on and off the job, and usually they receive no extra payment. If you think it can't be done in the West, I have news for you. Northrop Industries adapted the Japanese concept of Quality Control Circles, (which I call Team Problem Solving), and in one situation alone saved $70,000 in lost time.

Sperry Vickers reports that in their very first pilot program the company saved more than $30,000 in product improvement and cost reduction. A number of Canadian companies are adapting the Team Problem Solving approach to their problems. Unfortunately, a few companies have rushed in and tried to set up a pilot program without properly understanding the principles involved. They succeeded in failing magnificently, and have abandoned the concept as "impractical and unworkable." The Bosses in these companies have not fully developed their A.Q. and consequently, they cannot achieve more than they think they can.

Leaders don't have this problem. They listen, learn, and experiment. They build on success, one step at a time. They don't rush in blindly and then blame the method because it doesn't work. I am not saying that all the methods used by Japanese industry would work in North America. But many could, and some are being adapted very successfully.

Leaders have a good A.Q., and remember: AQ plus IQ equals Effectiveness. One leader in particular whom I admire is John Sandford of DeHavilland Aircraft Corporation. He is the Chief Executive Officer, and I have had the privilege of working with his managers quite extensively over the past couple of years.

After a board meeting at DeHavilland, John Sandford holds a meeting in the company cafeteria to brief employees on what is new and what is going on. He is a great believer in Vitamin I (Information) and he makes sure that all of his employees are persons, and not pygmies.

In Japanese management, the stretching and growing of people and profits go together; one without the other does not make sense and would not work. Bosses who are running corporate dinosaurs into the ground are not yet aware of this fact.

The Japanese have proved that people feel their best when they are doing their best. They practice the art of stretching and growing people because they know that when people stop growing mentally, they start to die . . . 'on the job'. How do they do it? They do it through the continuous training of all employees at all levels.

This means that in a Japanese company all employees are constantly learning something new, not only in his job, but in all levels of his job. A janitor and an engineer will be required to attend training programs concerning every part of the plant in which they work. Peter Drucker reports that during one of his visits to Japan he was informed by a company president that he could not attend a certain meeting because he had to take part in a company welding course — as a student . . . not as an observer.

There is little doubt that the Japanese excel in teaching employees how to manage themselves. They are teaching the West a terrible and bitter lesson: if corporations don't practice the art of developing persons, they can never hope to optimize the full use of human and physical resources, nor to compete effectively in the 1980s.

So, what does it all add up to? How can we start to become more aware? A Zen Master might say "Don't think, look first." Become AWARE of what is going on around you. This is a constant theme of Zen and is rooted in Japanese thinking. Look around you. Do you tend to see things in terms of differences or similarities? Remember, in the final analysis, it is the difference that makes the difference, especially when you are growing people. Develop a yen for Zen. Read a few books on the subject. Stretch your A.Q.

In the next two decades there will be three kinds of employees: the quick, the dead, and the dying. The dying have two speeds: stop and dead slow . . . have you noticed? Wake-Up and become Aware. Think about it. A yen for Zen might help you to survive.

CHAPTER IX

Prophets and Profits

Are you making tomorrow happen? Do you know HOW to make tomorrow happen? Anticipating the future, and then making it happen, should figure prominently in your behavior as a manger because — quite literally — your job is to make the future happen — tomorrow, next week, next month, next year. How much time per day do you invest in making tomorrow happen? Not too sure? . . . Or maybe none? All right. I have news for you: If you are not investing 10 — 15% of your time per day in making tomorrow happen, I don't care what the sign says on your desk or on your door, you are not a manager — you are just the highest paid worker in your department.

Planning, that much-maligned and misunderstood function, is looking ahead to see what's coming up . . . down the road. Are you looking ahead? Leaders do. Bosses don't. That's why Bosses manage by crisis, constantly urging and purging their pygmies to work harder and harder. Interestingly enough, the harder they work, the fewer results they seem to get. They have become classic victims of the activity trap, unwittingly set and sprung by Bosses who have a blind spot when it comes to differentiating between effeciency and effectiveness.

To stay healthy, the corporate body must stretch and grow and be capable of absorbing the impact of Super-Shock. How can a corporate body do that? For starters, have you ever heard of the Delphi technique? If you are in marketing . . . you sure have. It's a pretty useful technique, and not hard to adapt to your industry or organization, whatever it is or does.

The fact is that this time next year you will not be exactly the same person you are today. Neither will your job, your company, nor your country. Change, change, change, is the predominant characteristic of our age. Corporate dinosaurs, suffering from a hardening of the categories, will fall like flies on a winter's day unless they develop their prophets and people, as well as profits.

The new breed of managerial Leaders know well how to harness human and physical resources to achieve goals and objectives.

The Bosses who run the corporate dinosaurs are running them into the ground because they do not understand the difference between running a corporation and managing one. Long and loud do they lament the fact that change has overtaken them; they did not read the future; they did not set out to *make* the future happen; they *let* the future happen. They ignored the needs of the little people in the market place, as well as in the workplace. Now they are taking a beating, and everyone must suffer. The final irony is that they now expect the government to pass legislation to put a halt to unfair competition. What happened to our red-blooded sons of free enterprise? They dozed off in the late 19th century, and like Rip Van Winkle are now just begining to awake. When the corporate giants of the auto industry admit they can't keep up with change, when they must recall hundreds of thousands of cars that are not safe at any speed, clearly, something is wrong.

Remember when you bought a car that turned out to be a lemon? You complained and you were ignored or given the run around. The dinosaurs have only contempt for pygmies.

The prophets of old attempted to predict the furture by consulting a variety of oracles. One of the most famous was the oracle of Delphi, which usually obliged its clients with ambiguous answers.

If you know anything abut marketing you will have heard of the so called Delphi technique, which is presently in vogue. You can adapt it successfully to your industry, whatever it is, and I recommend this particular procedure to any organization interested in de-hardening its categories and making the future happen.

What you do is this: Call together half a dozen representatives of your industry or company and invite them to spend the next three months (full-time if possible) researching, independently of each other, the likely developments in your field over the next ten years. On a given date, these persons should gather and independently table their reports. From these reports it is possible to develop a probability curve in terms of what is likely to happen in the future that will affect your industry — based on well-researched guestimates. The next step is to develop a scenario around the probabilities affecting your interests, rather like writing a movie script. Everything is fleshed out in terms of people, what they will likely be doing, wearing, eating, and so on. Having developed a Three-D picture of the future, it is then possible to set objectives, develop plans, and make the future happen. As Peter Drucker has pointed out, "For the first time in history it is possible to make the future happen."

Futurists in management keep in mind that people do not attempt things they cannot achieve . . . and so they seldom achieve more than they think they can. Futurists are the modern prophets. Like Buckminster Fuller, they make the future happen. Think of the geodesic dome now in use around the world. Fuller showed the world how to do more with less, and progressive, healthy corporations are doing the same in many fields: computers, television cables, optic fibres, and so on.

Question: Are there any prophets in your organization planning to make the future happen for you? Or is your outfit full of Bosses hypnotized by the rear-view mirror?

Remember: Profits without prophets will not guarantee your survival.

An ancient prophet once said:

God gave us two ends with a connecting link;
One to sit on, the other to think.
Success depends on which end you use,
Heads you win . . . Tails you lose.

CHAPTER X

The Great Ponos

Let me ask you this question? What do you mean by that old-fashioned, four letter word spelled W-O-R-K? To most people, including Bosses, work just means work. But what does it really mean? The ancient Greeks had a word for work: *PONOS*, which means sorrow. The Hebrew word for work means punishment, or atonement for original sin. Eventually, Luther preached that work is the way to serve God, and later the Calvinists believed that all work was God's work. Such was the evolution of the meaning of work which gave rise to the so-called Protestant work ethic: "work is good, idleness is evil."

In a fascinating, two year study the Upjohn Institute issued a report entitled, *Work in America*. It was published in 1973, and in the report work was defined as, "an activity that produces something of value to other people." The study points out that the confusion of pay with work goes back to the historic distinction between 'noble' and 'ignoble' tasks. A person without work is 'worthless'. For centuries the economic and social importance of work colored our thinking, and little or no attention was paid to the personal meaning of work.

An operational definition of work must include two ingredients: 1) an activity that requires mastery of some part of our environment, mental or physical, and 2) an activity that is of value to others. Note that nothing is said about money, wages, or salary. This definition takes in a wide territory and recognizes, for example, that unpaid activities performed by mothers, volunteers, etc., is very definitely work. Behavioral research shows quite convincingly that the work people do is critical in terms of what it contributes to self-esteem.

What makes us tick, according to Dr. David McLelland of Harvard University, is the way we see ourselves as we would like to be. Most people like to feel that what they do is important and valued by their employer. Leaders are constantly striving to make sure their employees have plenty of Vitamin I (Information) regarding the importance and value of their work. Bosses think this sort of thing is a waste of time. They don't realize that their people have become pygmies, and are psychologically starving to death right under their noses. Psycho-vitamin deficiency in the daily diet of work is the source of the great Ponos, or sorrow in work, that afflicts untold numbers of people in the world of work today.

When I want to run a quick check on the quality of work-vitamins in any organization, all I have to do is ask employees a few questions: "Do you know how much that steel chisel costs?" "No idea." "It costs $14." "You're kidding, I didn't know they cost that much!"

"Do you know how much it would cost to replace that lathe you are working on?" "No idea." "$75,000." "Gee, I didn't know."

"Do you know the dollar value that *your* work adds to the product?" "No idea." Very often when I tell them they say things like: "Gee I didn't realise my work was that important, and they look surprised and pleased.

The importance of attitude toward work becomes obvious in these common, everyday situations. How can an employee respect his work or himself if he is deprived of basic information regarding its value. In a Japanese factory bulletins on costs, production schedules, and work problems are abundantly displayed and discussed by work teams. Japanese workers are expected to manage themselves and solve their own day-to-day problems. They develop respect for their work and respect for themselves.

Dr. William James, a brilliant and famous psychologist, said, "The greatest discovery of our generation is the knowledge that by changing a man's attitude we can change his life." Leaders know that the success or failure of a corporation is determined more by the attitudes of their people than by their ability or anything else.

If an employee has a good attitude, he will get good results. If he has a poor attitude, he will get poor results. In the final analysis, employees evaluate themselves in terms of the work they do. Meaningful work, therefore, is work that develops a positive self-image based on worth. Poor performance is the product of a poor self-image, an image of worthlessness.

It adds up to this: across North America there are countless employees suffering from the great sorrow inherent in their work. In a sense, they are dying on the job, or have already retired. I sometimes think I am in the business of resurrection.

A large corporation in Toronto decided to move all of its staff to a larger building. After years of complaints from numerous pygmies about inadequate space and other problems, the Bosses decided to put up a brand new head office right in the middle of town. All the details were carefully planned by an imposing committee of Bosses and architects. When the pygmies were finally moved in . . . guess what happened? They came up with more complaints than ever. Why? because the Bosses had not bothered to consult them in any way regarding their needs. In the first few weeks after the opening ceremonies, it was not uncommon for a visitor to observe employees running up and down stairs muttering to themselves about the stupidity of the Bosses for misplacing washrooms, storage rooms, and elevators. Were they ever mad. So were the Bosses.

Contrast these events with what happened in another company which employed about two hundred men. The plant had become outdated and conditions were cramped. The Leaders decided to build a new plant not too far away. Before a stone was turned in the ground, the men were invited to visit the new site in groups of about twenty to hold meetings with the architects. Each meeting started off with the plant manager saying: "You fellows know the problems we have been having in the old plant, and we want your help in designing a new plant that will help you to do a better job. The architects are here to listen to you and make notes on your suggestions. You will be meeting with them from time to time to offer your advice. You are all on the team."

You should have seen the action! When these guys returned to the old plant for lunch, instead of playing cards and fooling around, they were arguing and drawing sketches on the back of old envelopes and saying things like: "Don't forget, Joe, next time we gotta remind the architects to make that gangway four feet wider." The men were excited, stimulated, and involved. They were offering invaluable ideas freely and anxiously, because they had a real stake in the outcome. They were stretching and growing and felt they were important. They were, in fact, partners and consultants. The best consultants a company can have are already on the payroll. Leaders know this, but Bosses don't. When the new plant was finally finished, the employees were encouraged to take visitors around and explain how it was designed. "See that bay over there, that was my idea. It gives us the back-up room we never had in the old place. Now we can turn around faster." They were pleased and they were proud. They were people, not pygmies, and they knew it.

A large, northern industrial plant threw out the assembly line process, put all their people on a salary basis, and assembled them in groups of six around their machines. This is what they were told: "If you guys can figure out a way of doing your job with only five people, we don't care if the sixth man goes home, goes fishing, or gets drunk. But remember, if the item you assemble is returned by a customer as unsatisfactory, you will have to fix it in your own time without pay."

In less than eighteen months, this company, which had been six million dollars in the red, made more than one million dollars in the black.

Whether you are in the red or the black, you can't afford to treat your people like pygmies. Dear Boss: Don't think — *look!* Look around you and see what is happening in organizations that lead the field. Awake and become aware. See what is happening to the managerial dinosaurs as they lumber across the corporate landscape. One Boss I knew, who could not wait to hear what he was going to say, next told me that all his people were on the pill. When I asked him what evidence he had to back up this statement, he said, "Because they never give birth to any new ideas." He was quite unaware that in the eyes of his employees *He* was the pill, and a bitter pill at that. They would never give him that extra 5% that he kept asking for. They just disappeared into their job descriptions and languished in the great Ponos.

What do you think would happen if every person in the world of work became just 5% more effective in doing his or her job. The overall effect on the economy would be staggering. What do you think would happen if every person in your company became just 5% more effective. You know, and I know. The roof would blow off.

The problem is, how can you get that extra 5%. We all know that everyone, including ourselves, could be at least 5% more effective in doing his work if he really wanted to. The interesting thing is that if you were to increase salaries or wages by 15 or 20%, there would be little or no improvement. People would assume that they had earned the increase on the basis of present performance. The fact recognized by Leaders, but not by Bosses, is that you cannot command or demand that extra 5%. And yet, it is there. Leaders can get it, but Bosses can't. In fact, Leaders can get very much more than 5% in many cases, because they understand that many employees are underemployed; they are not fully utilized.

Think about the person you work for. Don't you often say to yourself: "I could do his job just as well as he does, if not better, or at least a part of it." And you would be right. How many people are looking up to you at work and say the same thing to themselves. And they are probably right. There is a lot of slack in the world of work which Bosses cannot control or reduce by 'motivation'. Leaders can reduce this kind of slack by creating a climate for self-control and self-motivation. They do it all the time. So can you, but first you must understand what is going on in the world of work.

Professor George Odiorne says there is no point in learning new management skills unless you also realize there is a whole new breed of cat moving into the work force in more ways than one. You can't apply management skills in a vacuum. If you do, nothing will happen.

CHAPTER XI

The Eleventh Commandment

In what has been described as a world's record, the 82,000 employees of Matsushita Electric turned in 663,475 written suggestions in one year for improving sales, cutting costs, and increasing productivity. This works out to about 8 suggestions per employee.

How did this corporation achieve such a fantastic volume of ideas from its employees? Because they were treated as people rather than pygmies. They were also given large doses of Psychovitamin therapy: Vitamin O for Opportunity, to grow on the job. Vitamin A for Achievement. And Vitamin R2 for Recognition.

Matsushita Electric is a lean, lithe, corporate body. It has come a long way from a $50 start. It has stretched and grown to a major, international corporation with 118 factories and more than $4.6 billion in sales.

President Masahara Matsushita's policy of "listening hard" is the eleventh commandment for any corporation wishing to overcome pygmyitis.

Matsushita listens hard not only to his employees but also to dealers and consumers as well. He does not sit in his office all day long, poring over field reports and statistical data. He believes in and practices something called MBWA, or Management By Walking About. He gets into the plant and the offices of his corporation and talks and listens to his people. He travels the world to listen to everyone involved in his operations. He does not sit back and take it for granted that he knows all the answers, and therefore does not have to listen. He knows that listening is the key that unlocks the doors of perception.

Matsushita tells his people, "You are working for yourselves." No wonder, then, that employees meet on their own time to discuss ways of improving productivity and product quality. As Maslow has pointed out, the need to belong is very strong. When there is a strong feeling of belonging, self-esteem and opportunity, people and profits will stretch and grow. The fact that we have two ears and only one mouth might suggest that we should listen twice as much as we talk. I would go even further and stress the need to listen nine times more than you talk, and ask three times as many questions as you give answers.

If you are a manager in the 1980s and you don't practice the eleventh commandment, you are a Boss and your pygmies will give you more problems than you can shake a stick at.

Have you noticed the full, two-page and single-page ads by Sperry Vickers in business magazines? Very interesting. Here is a good example of a healthy corporate body revealing the secret of its success through the practice of the eleventh commandment. Their ads say: "KNOWING HOW

TO LISTEN TAKES MORE THAN TWO GOOD EARS." It takes Listening. Sperry employs more than 87,000 employees, and provides courses in listening for personnel from around the world, including the chairman of the board. Sperry points out that listening can make the difference that makes the difference between poor and outstanding results.

Corporations that believe in helping their people to learn more about the difference between hearing and listening are free from all the symptoms of pygmyitis. Why? Because, when people are listened to, they start to listen to themselves, and gain insight into their potential for contribution and personal growth.

Some ancient wisdom. In Egypt, 4,400 years ago, one of the Pharaohs instructed tax collectors to listen to the pleas of the people, and to listen patiently and without rancour, because, "a person wants attention to what he says even more than the granting of his wish."

Listening has been called "Action Research" by management consultants who are serious in their practice of the 11th commandment. They know that, contrary to common belief, listening is a dynamic, not a passive process. Bosses think that listening is a sign of weakness, when actually it is a sign of great strength. By careful listening, a Leader can hear much that will enable him to respond to a speaker with wisdom and meaning, and this will be to their mutual benefit.

The need for improved communication has often been stressed by Bosses because corporate dinosaurs are plagued at all levels with endless breakdowns in understanding. Bosses do not understand that the real art of communication lies not in how things are said but in getting people to listen. Bosses frequently tell me that they don't want to listen to their employees; they want employees to listen to them. Listening — real listening — takes courage and strength. Most Bosses are afraid to listen because someone might persuade them to change their minds. Of course, silence is not always golden. Silence is not necessarily listening. The difference between hearing and listening is easily portrayed by the man and wife scenario at the breakfast table. Hubby is reading the sports page and his wife is talking. Suddenly she says, "You are not listening," and hubby replies, "I can hear you, keep talking."

True listening means making it possible for people to talk with themselves, because, by so doing, they often gain insight into their problems and find a solution. Psychiatrists know this and so do women. Women are usually better listeners than men because, like psychiatrists, they get a lot of practice, although this is changing. Bosses convert people into pygmies by never listening to what people have to say. They hear, but they don't listen. Leaders practice the Eleventh commandment!

Listen Unto Others
As You Would Have Them Listen
Unto You

CHAPTER XII

The Educational Dinosaur

If you were asked whether you think we are moving toward full employment or full unemployment, you would have to admit that the latter is by far the more likely. How come? Why is it that in countries like Canada and the United States, with their vast resources and almost limitless opportunities, millions of our people are unemployed? One reason is that the corporate dinosaurs of education are looking into the rear-view mirror. They are still geared to the curriculum of the past, and the curriculum of the past is just that — past. Many of the Bosses of educational dinosaurs need a dose of Zen and needle pie. The curriculum of the future must be the future. In other words, educators should be looking ahead and developing curriculums that will enable people to survive in a post-industrial era. Too many schools and colleges today are simply cookie cutters for the corporate dinosaurs of business, industry, and government. Designed on 19th century assembly line principles, they take in raw young people at one end and churn out mass-produced conformists at the other end. The whole concept of education, in terms of learning for learning's sake, has gone down the tube. It is common knowledge that at many of our so-called universities it is possible to attend for three years and graduate without ever having spoken to a professor. No wonder some graduating students have ripped up their diplomas in contempt. Pygmies for the market place seems to be the unspoken strategy of the educational dinosaurs.

The fact is, there are not enough jobs for thousands of young people in North America, and those available require skills which the dinosaurs of education have failed to provide.

Education has been segregated from instead of integrated with the world of work. The skilled workers required for the economy have, for the most part, been imported from Europe. In increasing numbers they are now retiring, and there is no one to take their place. The mindless neglect of technical and managerial skills by the educational dinosaurs has not only created a deficit of leadership in those areas, it has created underemployment for thousands of educated people in the work place. In my opinion, underemployment is a far more serious problem than unemployment in terms of the frustration, waste, and alienation it creates.

The educational dinosaurs know nothing and have done nothing to create awareness of new needs in the work place in a rapidly changing society. The explosion of knowledge is creating many new forms of employment and reducing the life expectancy of each. *The Dictionary of Occupations and Titles in Canada* lists more than 45,000 jobs to choose from, and the number of new occupations is growing all the time. A young person leaving school today can expect to change his or her occupation at least three times in a lifetime, perhaps more. What are the educational dinosaurs doing about that? Not a blessed thing that makes sense. Instead of teaching young people to think clearly, write clearly, and speak clearly, they are teaching them how to make cookies, make clothes, watch movies, play games, and go on field trips with no stated purpose. This is not education, and it most certainly is not vocational training. Whatever high-sounding purpose these activities may have in the cortical connections of the dinosaurs, the tragic truth, in fact, is that they are producing mindless conformists for the corporate dinosaurs of business, industry, and government.

Mindless conformity in the schools breeds mindless conformity in the world of work, which in turn breeds Bosses by the barrelfull. It is only when young people start to mature that they question the inanities of the corporate dinosaurs. As things are at present, very few of them will be fortunate to find themselves working for a Leader in a forward-looking, results-oriented organization.

Learning a living is going to be a permanent process, and the goal of all learning for most people will be not so much to get ahead, but to stay where they are. Professionals in every field today are going back to school for just that purpose. Those that don't . . . don't last.

The inescapable fact is that the educational dinosaurs have proved to be incapable of responding to the needs of the world of work, and this has resulted in a vast amount of overtraining and underemployment. On top of this, Bosses have fallen into the trap of looking for higher and higher qualifications to do ritual or routine jobs. They prefer paper to performance.

In spite of billions spent to improve education, we still have the wrong mix to meet the needs of the post-industrial era. The truth that seems to elude the cortical connections of the educational dinosaurs is that education must be future focussed to meet the needs of PEOPLE, not pygmies.

Corporate dinosaurs view a college diploma as more important than a good education. Hence, the mad and mindless rush to acquire a diploma, a certificate, anything that will please and appease a rear-view-mirror boss with a great future behind him.

With thousands of diploma holders unable to find employment relevant to their education, one can only marvel at the insanities of the educational supermarkets. The Maginot mentality of educational dinosaurs is clearly revealed by the refusal of certain colleges to invite Buckminster Fuller, Eric Hoffer, or Andrew Wyeth to lecture, because they never went to college. Other colleges, in contrast, are prepared to admit students into their graduate schools who never attended high school.

I have met a number of university graduates who are driving a cab for a living, not out of choice, but out of necessity. At the same time, there are thousands of men and women in the world of work who have made highly successful and important contributions to the country or the economy who do not possess a college diploma. Through pure intelligence, persistence — or what Dr. David McLelland of Harvard calls, "the need to achieve," they have, in the words of Peter Drucker, followed "parallel paths of achievement" and they have produced results. (*The Age of Discontinuity*)

Discrimination by education is a fact of life in-corporate dinosaurs today, and yet the imprint of seal on parchment in no way guarantees value to society or the economic system.

Writing in *The Age of Discontinuity* (p. 332), Peter Drucker expresses the hope that requests for information on schooling in job applications will be made illegal. He upbraids corporations that overlook talent already on the payroll; individuals who may have been outstanding performers for years and yet denied promotion for lack of a piece of paper. He reminds us that it was Napoleon who, after every victory, asked, "Où sont les braves?" Soldiers who excelled in battle, regardless of rank or education, were promoted on the spot.

Discrimination against proven performers in the workplace creates a caste system that essentially confines them to pygmy status. If they can't get on, they will very often get out and join a results-oriented outfit where they are paid for performance. Sometimes they start up something on their own, and do very well indeed.

There is quite a bit of evidence to suggest that there is not much connection between diplomas and on-the-job performance. Bosses live under the illusion that paper indicates potential. But the fact is that Leaders don't pay for potential, they pay for results.

When you realize that thousands and thousands of students are, at this very minute, being trained for jobs which don't exist, it becomes painfully apparent that many of our educational dinosaurs are floundering in chaos and confusion, to say nothing of declining enrolments. Currently, they compete for anyone who breathes. Body count is big on campus these days. The almighty dollar comes first.

A massive study conducted by Columbia University, under the superbly appropriate title, *Education & Jobs — The Great Training Robbery*, found no connection between degrees and performance in many occupations. In fact, the study revealed that in many jobs people who had no degrees did a better job.

In my work with corporations of all kinds I often come across non-diploma employees who outperform their diplomaed colleagues. For some mysterious reason they are often considered to be inferior. In discussing this with Bosses, I have frequently been told that employees who have a diploma have proved that they are stable and capable of conforming to an institutional environment. I remember meeting a woman in Toronto who did outstanding work for handicapped children. Many of the professionals in her field regarded her as a crackpot because she had never been to a university. "How could she possibly know anything," they said. To them she was a pygmy. To the parents and children she assisted, she was a giant.

In 1971 the Supreme Court of the United States ruled against the right of an employer to demand a diploma unless it could be shown that it could reliably predict results on the job. The last I heard was that the ruling is still being appealed. If the day comes when employees challenge employers successfully on this issue, employers will have to think through what is, and what is not, relevant to success on a given job.

Back in the 60s and 70s it must have been obvious to the educational dinosaurs of our land that the demand for teachers was going to fade in the 80s. Did they take the trouble to point this out to students. Of course not. It would have undermined their budgets.

Now, in the 80s, we have the spectacle of teachers driving taxis, teachers doing typing, and teachers killing time. Many of these young teachers have become bitter and feel diminished, not only in their expectations, but in their self-image. Most will be converted into pygmies somewhere in the world of work, and many will wind up doing a dumb job. A dumb job does not mean a dumb person is doing it, but unfortunately there are more dumb jobs than there are dumb people. This is a terrible waste of trained human resources in the world of work created by cowardly Bosses who decided that discretion is the better part of valor.

On May 4, 1981, *Time* magazine devoted a front page cover and lead article entitled, "The Money Chasers — Business School Solutions May Be A Part Of The US Problem," in a sobering evaluation of that much-vaunted symbol of managerial status, the MBA. According to *Time*, the MBA is being devalued by overproduction and the inability of its holders to produce results in the sticky areas of management. "A lot of what is preached at business schools today is absolute rot" according to Michael Thomas, a New York financial consultant. "It is paper management," he is quoted as saying, "it is not the management of hard resources and people. Business schools teach that business is nothing but numbers — and the numbers only for the next quarter." Getting results in the short-term has become a characteristic of a good deal of management in the United States, and this has a number of foreign observers worried.

I shall never forget being invited to talk with a group of key managers employed by one of the largest and best known corporations in the world. At one point I asked the group what they considered to be their most important responsibility as managers. "Numbers," they assured me, in hushed and reverential tones, "Numbers, of course." Many or most were MBAs. *PEOPLE*, had not occurred to them.

Jerry Harvey, professor of management at George Washington University, was also quoted in the *Time* article: "We've designed organizations that reward people who think very narrowly. Why aren't management textbooks funny? It's because they don't have much realism to them. If they had much realism to them, they'd be funny as hell."

It seems we are confronted with an ironic fact: many of the schools of business education are dinosaurs that are guilty of producing a very special breed of pygmy into the world of work. According to executives quoted in *Time*, they are, "arrogant amateurs, trained only in figures and lacking experience in both the manufacture of goods and the handling of people."

Most of the MBAs I have met have turned out to be bright, personable, and articulate people who seem to be doing a good job in most respects. It's true that they are seldom found involved in the smoke and fury of front-line management, and that may well be their Achilles heel, when the chips are down.

In Canada, W. Dimma, president of A.E. Lepage in Toronto and former dean of management education at York University, is quoted as saying, "Business Schools have problems getting students to take courses in manufacturing and production. That's not a popular area any more." (*Canadian Business*, February 1981.)

If business schools and corporate dinosaurs are failing to produce Leaders who effectively manage people, where do we turn for help?

I believe we have to reflect upon the Napoleonic formula for success, and ask ourselves: What do Leaders do? In effect, to paraphrase Napoleon, they ask not, "where are the heroes," but, "who has produced excellence?" Not all outstanding performers are good at training, but many are. They should be given rotating assignments in training departments to assist in the coaching and counselling of supervisors and managers. And they should do this on the job, not stuck away in a classsroom environment. Of course, it is necessary to have talks and discussions in a conference room, but training in a practical situation, for example in running a meeting, can be done on the job and critiqued by a peer group afterward.

Management development and developing managers are, as Drucker points out, two different but related tasks. The first is concerned with the growth of the corporate body as a whole, the second is concerned with the growth of individual managers. (*Management*, p. 425.)

Management development looks ahead and tries to predict the categories of human resources required to handle changing needs in changing markets.

Developing managers is concerned with ways and means to encourage managers to stretch and grow so they can get things done effectively through other people.

I remember hearing George Odiorne, the father of MBO, say one time at the University of Wisconsin, that in developing managers it is important to do something totally unrelated to their usual everyday routines in order to shake up their mind set. At one of his seminars for managers, he conducted a worm cutting experiment. Run some worms through a maze, select the fastest, cut them up and feed them to the rest of the worms, and then re-run the test and measure the speed of the survivors. They were always faster. His point was, of course, that there is no use in jogging the body if you don't jog the mind. I have discovered that most Bosses think that management development is something to do with attending courses on management. Attending courses is only a small part of manager development in any truly successful program. Studies show that outstanding Leaders in management attribute their success to learning on the job under an outstanding superior. Someone who was willing to listen, encourage, and permit them the opportunity to make mistakes.

Few Bosses are clear on the difference between training and development. Leaders are. A new employee undergoing training is aware that he needs training, and the technique used is called coaching, just as in sports. When a new employee has reached a minimal standard of importance, he is then ready for development. He may be unaware of his need for development to a higher level of performance, or he may lack confidence. At this point a Leader uses a technique called counselling. This involves helping an employee to evaluate his performance in light of personal and corporate goals. Not many managers are good at this. Japanese managers are. This is their great strength in dealing with people. Bosses rarely admit their need for training, and, as for development, they just don't need it, of course. They remind me of Nietzsche's words: "Too well do I know those God-like ones; they insist on being believed in, and that doubt is sin. Too well do I know what they themselves most believe in."

The ultimate challenge to schools of management education is to provide guidelines within which the rituals of work can be transformed into meaningful experiences in living. Bosses who inhabit the political institutions of education need to be reminded of a remark attributed to Bismarck: "It's easy enough to find a Minister of Education: all the job needs is a long white beard. But a good cook is different; that requires universal genius."

CHAPTER XIII

People Make Profits

THE ZIPPER KING

Tadao Yoshida was a schoolboy in Japan in the 1920s when he became inspired by an aphorism attributed to the late Andrew Carnegie: "Unless you render profit and goodness to others you cannot prosper."

Now sixty-five years of age, Yoshida heads YKK, the world's largest zipper manufacturing company. Throughout his life he has assiduously applied Carnegie's principle which is, in effect, that PEOPLE MAKE PROFITS.

In 1974 Yoshida's company produced 500,200 miles of zippers, which would have reached the moon and back. In the same year Yoshida anticipated a profit of $56 million dollars.

Who said people don't make profits? According to *Time*, Yoshida's sales grew from $170.00 in 1934 to $475 million in the 70s, and are expected to reach the magic $ billion sometime in the 80s.

Yoshida invests one third of his profit in keeping prices down, one third in rebates and discounts to customers, and one third he keeps as 'pure' profit.

It turns out that employees keep more of the profits than Yoshida himself. The 1300 employees in Japan own two thirds of the stock on a profit sharing basis, and this opportunity will be extended to YKK employees around the world, including Canada, the U.S., and twenty-seven other countries.

Not a bad record for a Leader who believes that People Make Profits. When employees become partners there is no limit to what may be achieved.

CHAPTER XIV

Growing Up On The Job

Pygmies in the world of work are the product of parent-child relationships with their Bosses. Bosses, quite unwittingly for the most part, get caught in a trap of their own making. All people grow up in some kind of parent-child relationship, until they reach maturity and become capable of managing themselves. Good parents want their children to grow up and go out into the world and manage themselves. They also expect their children to relate to them as adults to adults. God help the child whose parents try to maintain a dependency relationship during the maturation process.

The good manager, like the good parent, wants his new employees to learn, grow, and mature until they can manage their work on their own most of the time.

Unconsciously, corporate dinosaurs implement a variety of policies and practices which maintain parent-child relationships, create frustration, and produce pygmies. Pygmies, remember, in the sense we are using the term, are employees who are treated like little children. If they are good, they will be rewarded, and if they are bad, they will be punished.

Let's take a look at some of these practices. For a start, think about the corporate or company newsletter for employees. A good idea in principle but it usually gets screwed up by a bunch of uptight Bosses who upset proceedings by editing the life out of anything vital, interesting, or controversial. Oh sure, they will invite employees to write in with their suggestions, and their questions, but what do they get? Nothing much. Pygmies learn from experience that there is no way they will get any response to any request for information that really interests them, so they don't bother to write in. The Boss committee and its editor will complain about employee apathy. There is a lot of apathy in the bowels of every corporate dinosaur. The upshot is that most employee newsletters churn out a pile of pre-digested pasteurized pap, totally unfit for people consumption, but ideal for pygmies. Take a look at any one of them, and what do you see: a child-like collage of corporate clichés, dutiful thanks, coy congratulations, and pictures of pygmies with frozen smiles. This kind of junk perpetuates the old parent-child relationship in an aura of condescension. Have you noticed large piles of company newsletters lying around at strategic points? They often lie around for weeks until just before the next edition is due, then they are surreptitiously removed. No one has bothered to pick them up, unless they need scrap paper in a hurry. One practical pygmy I knew — he was a neighbor of mine who had permanently retired on his job — used to collect newsletters from his company in bundles to light fires at home. "Light Up And

Smile" was the title of these masterpieces. They lit up his life all right. As he put it: "Reading them is a pain, but burning them is a pleasure." He told me some time later that the Boss committee of the newsletter was conducting an extensive survey to find out why people were not interested in contributing letters to the committee. The Boss committee was concerned because, as they explained in an editorial, "This is YOUR newsletter!"

Newsletters and other company periodicals that emanate from healthy companies that lead the field are produced in a quite different manner. Volunteer reporters are recruited from all levels of the organization and work as a team with a good editor who is also a good Leader. They are encouraged to forage for facts concerning issues that truly concern employees in their own unit or section. These are printed, very often in full, with answers from top management in the everyday language of the employees concerned. No fooling around. In one company I know, it is not uncommon to find the front page is devoted to question raised by an employee and the back page will carry an answer from the president. He levels with his people and they respect and admire him for it. I have often seen him shirt-sleeving with employees in different parts of the office and plant. He just wanders around practicing MBWA (Management By Walking Around); he will drop in on a group without warning and ask: "What could I do that would help you do a better job?" You should see the loyalty in that company; you can almost feel it.

I don't know how vacancies are filled at your place, but I do know how they are filled in a lot of corporate dinosaurs. First of all, employees have to get permission from their Boss before they can bid on any job that becomes vacant. In a number of cases, employees are not always notified of jobs that become available. The crowning insult occurs when an employee who wins a new position inside the company is prevented from moving for weeks or months because his or her Boss complains that they can't be spared. An application for a transfer to another department will often be seen by a Boss as an insult. Why would someone want to move out from my department? is the unspoken question that bugs them. I have known Bosses who deliberately stalled in releasing an employee just in order to needle and humiliate them. "We're not good enough for you, I suppose," is an example of the kind of statement that can greet someone who dares to move.

Leaders don't play games with their people. They encourage learning, growth, and mobility wherever possible. Employees are permitted to apply for other jobs without informing their supervisors. If they are successful, they must be released within ten days.

Leaders are very much aware that their number one responsibility is to train and develop their people. Naturally, there will come a time when a good employee wants to move up the ladder. A Leader will encourage this upward movement. A Boss will discourage it in every way he can.

If I want to find out where the first class managers are in a corporation, all I have to do is to ask the personnel department to tell me where most of the promotions are coming from. Wherever they are coming from, they are coming from a department or a division where there is one hell of a good manager.

When a Boss loses a good employee he beefs

that now he has to start all over and train somebody else. Leaders accept the fact that, above anything else, they are developers of people. Bosses tend to be reluctant to develop a back-up person, and they are notorious for withholding information and opportunities to fail. They don't delegate because they are afraid someone might take their job. Occasionally I say to a senior executive: "Why don't you promote so and so?" The answer I get is: "Hell, we can't promote him, there is no one to take his place." And so this fearful Boss is passed over in favor of someone else, and he never knows it happened.

Another characteristic of the flagging dinosaur is its KGB-like control of information. Everything is very hush hush, and strictly classified into 'Confidential', 'Classified', 'Top Secret', 'Managers Only' or 'Salaried Personnel'. Too much classification of information not only creates a Vitamin I (Information) deficiency, it creates a hardening of the categories as well. When was the last time you had a medical checkup? No, I am serious. It's just possible your doctor told you to watch out because you are developing a hardening of the arteries. He made you aware of a condition that could prove to be fatal if left untreated. Bosses are quite unaware that a hardening of the categories can and does prove fatal to corporate dinosaurs, if not treated in time. Dehardening cortical categories is step number one for any consultant or Leader who is assigned to a corporate dinosaur to administer treatment.

Management by perception becomes the most important priority in retraining Bosses at all levels. Oh yes, and you would be surprised if you knew how many dinosaurs are undergoing massive multimegaton therapy right now. You won't read about it in the headlines, of course. But it is happening, all right. The sad part about it is that in most cases it is happening too late to save the patients. Don't blame the doctor if you neglect your aches and pains for years and then find yourself listening to the last rites. Many a corporate dinosaur, right today, is frantically plugging its ears because it doesn't want to hear the terrible truth: the corporate graveyard looms ever closer and deathbed confessions are made by desperate Bosses who plead for access to the public trough to bail them out, before the bailiffs move in. Absolution may be possible, but redemption and salvation seldom are.

Corporate dinosaurs never permit employees to have access to their files. Healthy corporations do. They are quite willing to share information on profits as well as costs and expenses. Bosses balk at the very idea of discussing profits with employees. Somehow, that is not quite respectable. But why not? Why is profit a dirty word, except among top Bosses? Because it is assumed that if employees know how much profit is being made, they will demand more pay.

The hostility manifested against business in our society today comes in large part because profit is not understood. Bosses have done a poor job in educating the community at large in the true meaning of profit. Most people assume that every company is in business to maximize profit. Dead wrong. Any company that tried to maximize profit in our society today would be put out of business in a hurry. They just can't do it. The old robber barons of fifty years ago could do it, and did do it. But today, well, just think of the constraints that are imposed on a company by a host of regulatory bodies. As Peter Drucker has pointed out many times, the first concern of a company is not the maximization of profit, it is the prevention of loss. (See *Practice of Management*, p. 47.) It is interesting to note that where employee representatives have been elected to the boards of directors of progressive corporations, they are often very surprised, and, in some cases, shaken, when they learn about the small percentage of profit that is actually earned. If information on profit is shared honestly and openly with employees, and if those profits are shared with those same employees, it does much to create self-motivation and interest in productivity. People are much more willing to stretch and grow if there is something in it for them. Make a bigger pie and get a bigger slice. Only about 2% of companies in Canada are into some form of profit sharing, compared with more than 20% in the United States. It pays off.

More than 60 companies across Canada have employee reps on the board of directors. They get all the dope on profits and feed-back the details to all employees.

One notorious corporate dinosaur recently waited until the death rattle could be heard across the nation, and then, in a paroxysm of panic, it saw fit to appoint the head of its union to sit on the board of directors in the hope that this would fire up the troops, or at least put some passion into the pygmies. This kind of blatant and cynical tokenism is a blot on the escutcheon of all progressive corporations who see employee representation as a meaningful contribution to improving morale and productivity. In my opinion it is downright offensive, and only a Boss-oriented outfit would try to impress its pygmies with a deathbed conversion to a faith in people. It will never work.

Leaders provide adequate information to employees in any way, shape, or form, that will help those employees to better understand what is going on, so that they can make a more specific and improved response to their work. The Cox Company, near Hamilton, has located a computer in the center of its plant, which any employee may use at any time to obtain information about any aspect of the company's operations, including profits. If you want to see self-motivated people at work under Leaders, you should see the people at Cox. Employees will often work, overtime, without pay, because of their deep interest in their work. Each work team has full responsibility to set its own work standards, pay, vacation times, and hire and fire its members. AND IT WORKS!

Theory X Bosses have been much discussed in management literature, and they are, of course, typical and plentiful in every corporate dinosaur, whether it be in the private, government, or voluntary sector. The X Boss displays all the symptoms of cortical constipation and what he most desperately needs is a good cortical catharsis to clear out the cobwebs and make way for a new Awareness. Most Bosses are not aware that what they look at is not what they see, it is what they believe. They tend to confuse inferences with facts, jump to false conclusions, and then act on them. This is downright dangerous as well as unjust, particularly when appraising human behavior. The boss always 'knows' when people are 'lazy', 'don't want to work' and 'can't be trusted'. So they are forever on the watch, like a cat watching mice. They spend, most of their time watching, checking, and controlling, and diminish their employees.

Leaders are strong adherents to the philosophy of Theory Y, as espoused by Douglas McGregor in his famous book, *The Human Side of Enterprise*. Why? Because Leaders don't want pygmies working for them, they want fully developed people. Why? Because fully developed people are happier and they get far better results. Robert Townsend, the author of *Up The Organization*, is one of the best known and most successful practitioners of Theory Y. When he took over the Avis Corporation it had not made a nickel profit in 13 years, and he was told he would have to get rid of just about everybody at head office because they were 'lazy', 'didn't like work', and 'couldn't be trusted'. In his book he explains how he set about to build a Theory Y organization based on the teachings of Douglas McGregor. In three years the Avis Corporation made $9 million dollars profit. And Townsend achieved this result with the same group of people who ran the company before he took over. You can't argue with success, and yet I often run across personnel managers and training managers who tell me in an offhand fashion that Doug McGregor's methods are 'old hat'. They are looking for something new; something that will work.

The Japanese are probably the most ardent practitioners of Theory Y on the face of the earth. They know how to make it work, and HOW. The Japanese are naturally oriented to Theory Y Leadership and practice it to the hilt. For example: no Japanese manager gives an order. If a Japanese manager has to give a direct command he has failed. A Japanese manager practices reason, logic, and persuasion, and deals with employees on an adult-to-adult basis. He accepts this as perfectly normal procedure. The North American manager still thinks it's revolutionary, permissive, wishy-washy, long-haired, sloppy — you name it. They still prefer pygmies to people. Why? Because they are easier to organize and control. Bosses need a yen for Zen. WAKE UP, look around and see what is happening. The Japanese are going to take over in North America. It may not be too long before many of us will be working for Japanese managers in banks, trust companies, factories, and offices. North American employees currently working for Japanese managers at SONY, JAL, YKK, do not see their managers as 'Bosses'; they see them as equals, and people they can talk to freely about personal and company problems.

Japanese managers are highly skilled in helping people to grow up on the job. There are no parent-child relationships where work is concerned. There is great concern for the welfare of employees and no one is ever laid off for economic reasons. Peer pressure is used to solve most disciplinary problems. At the Toyota plant in Japan, there is no distinction between office workers and production workers in terms of salaries and benefits. With bonus, the average worker will make about $30-35,000, so let's not assume that 'cheap labor' is the secret weapon in Japanese industry. By the way, sixty-year-old workers at Toyota get a lump sum of around $60,000 when they retire.

The Japanese philosophy of developing people is based on what they call "The Cycle of Goodness." Japanese companies believe in being good for their people because they know their people will be good for them. The equivalent concept in the West is the

"Golden Mean." The only difference is that the Japanese not only believe it, they practice it. East and West are moving closer and closer, in more ways than one. Could it be that "do unto others" is now the key to economic survival?

CHAPTER XV

Men Underground

In *The Report of The Royal Commission on Health & Safety of Workers in Mines*, published in June, 1976, Professor J. Ham, who was chairman of the commission, quoted Frederic LePlay, a distinguished French sociologist and Inspector-General of Mines in France: "The most important thing to come out of the mines is the miner." Professor Ham stated that he shares that conviction, and so do I.

Many years ago I worked underground in the silver, lead, gold, and uranium mines of Australia and Canada. The treatment of men underground down through the ages is a classic example of the master-slave, Boss-servant, parent-child relationship in the world of work. In terms of courage, endurance, and physique the men underground are very far from being pygmies, but in terms of their treatment by the corporate dinosaurs of mining, they have often been treated worse than animals by ignorant, and sometimes brutal Bosses.

Under Professor J. Ham's inspiring leadership,

127 recommendations were made to improve the working conditions of men underground.

The right to refuse to work in dangerous conditions is one of the recommendations that stands out in my mind. If you have helped to carry out the broken body of a man crushed by rock fall, you would know how I feel. If you knew that this particular man had reported the loose rock above his drilling points to his Boss, and if you knew that this particular man had been told to "get in there, or get fired," you would know even better how I feel. Too many Bosses have been in the habit of assigning men to work under dangerous conditions in order to speed up production.

One time I was assigned to work in a certain part of a well known uranium mine in Ontario. I asked my Boss about the radiation level. I wanted to know if it was safe to work there. "Let me worry about the radiation son," he said, "you just do your job." Later, he told me that the average level of radiation throughout the mine was well within safety standards. And so it was. However, what my Boss did not tell me was that where I was working the radiation level was more than ten times above the safety level. William Jennings Bryan once said, "You shall not crucify mankind upon a cross of gold." I wonder how many men will be crucified upon a cross of uranium? How many miners will die a lingering death from continuous exposure to radioactive ore bodies? I wonder. In the short term, uranium cities in Canada were a paradise for pygmies. They were paid high wages and they asked no questions. No one told them anything. They had to find out the hard way. And eventually, many of them did.

Sometimes we'd ask our Bosses for information about what was going in the mines, what was being planned, and how would it affect us. We were told to mind our own business and get on with our work. If anyone complained about the food or accommodation he was given a timetable for departing buses.

Underground Bosses were never given any training in management, and they knew nothing about handling people. They were strictly order givers, and a miner was simply a pair of hands. If a pair of hands were injured, the owner was cast out on the scrap heaps of humanity and left to rot. The Bosses operated in a strictly boss-servant fashion. They were often negligent of worker safety by allowing unqualified employees to operate equipment, sometimes with little or no experience.

Section 169(14) of the Royal Commission's Report now states: "Every manager shall ensure that no person (note the word "person") works without supervision at any machine unless the person a) has received adequate training and instruction in the operation of the machine and any dangers connected therewith b) has recieved adequate supervision by a person having thorough knowledge and experience with the machine c) is capable of safely operating the machine without supervision."

If the Royal Commission saw fit to bring in a total of 127 recommendations to improve the lot of the men underground, perhaps you can imagine, just a little, how bad things really are down there in the bowels of the earth. If you have never been underground, I would recommend that you take a tour sometime. It is a highly educational experience, and it will make a lasting impression on the seat of your understanding, especially if you happen to think that miners are overpaid. Also, you will understand why there is a desperate shortage of miners across this land. No miner I have ever known would want his son to follow in his footsteps. Unnecessary exposure of employees to toxic substances, poisonous gases, loss of hearing, dangerous explosives, unsafe equipment, and inadequate safety procedures, all reveal the appalling indifference and contempt for some of the bravest and most important men in the world of work.

On page 172 of the Report, Professor Ham stresses that supervisors underground must "have the capacity for leadership." And, "The Commission strongly believes that the competence, morale, and leadership of the first-line supervisor is crucial to the effectiveness of the internal system of direct responsibility for the performance of work. Leadership throughout the internal system is the force which binds it together." The Commission noted that "the morale of shift bosses [foremen] may be undermined by senior supervision [bosses], both through their unresponsiveness to reported anomalous conditions and through downgrading his authority by their intervening in his area of responsibility."

Such behavior, of course, is typical of Bosses everywhere, and it is a daily occurrence in many well known mines in Canada. It is part of the underground work culture which keeps people in the dark in more ways than one. Underground Bosses who treat miners like mushrooms need to remember that mushrooms grow up and move toward the light. With the advent of the Royal

Commission's report, the men underground have glimpsed a light at the end of a very long tunnel. They know that things are begining to change.

Among other things, the Commission observed that present methods of instruction are characterized by 1) "lack of relevance to the organizational structure as it is understood by first line supervisors 2) inconsistency with attitudes of management and senior supervisors as these appear to the first line supervisor (foreman) 3) obscurity in the manner or means whereby the chain of responsibility is integrated 4) incompatibility between the theory of supervision and experience in practice."

This is indeed a scathing indictment of the current chaos, confusion, and obfuscation that prevails in the corporate dinosaurs of the mining industry. People, real live people have been, and still are badly used and abused. Do you know how many people have been killed in mines during the last ten years? And listen, I am talking about people, real live people who eat, drink, pay taxes, vote, watch TV, drive cars, buy homes, go to church, and go to bed, just like you and me. It's tragic, but it's true: the corporate dinosaurs of the mining industry are still in the Dark Ages when it comes to handling its most precious resources: people.

Thank you Professor Ham, and all those who assisted you in a gargantuan task. You have helped to light a way out of darkness for the men underground. Like you and me, they want to be people, not pygmies. I salute you.

CHAPTER XVI

Anyone You Know?

(TWO BOSSES AND TWO BEERS)

Jack: "Hell, I dunno Jim, I have so much work coming across my desk every day: schedules, requests for transfers, performance appraisals, articles to read, monthly budget figures to go over. I can never catch up."

Jim: (Nods sympathetically and sips his beer.) "I know, Jack, I have exactly the same problems. I just didn't realize what I was letting myself in for when I became a manager. 'You're a manager now,' they said, 'so go out there and manage.' Big deal. 'Get the work out and keep costs down!' That's what they said. Sink or swim, and that was it."

Jack: "Right on, Jim, when I took over I knew something about handling costs, but I knew nothing about management; I just managed by instinct, by guess, and by God, you know. Obey orders and work hard, that's my philosophy. I don't know what's wrong with this outfit lately, we used to have things under control a while back . . . but now, phew, the way things are going there's just too much happening all at once. We just can't seem to find people to do Joe-jobs anymore, and as for skilled help, forget it."

Jim: "That's right, and you know something, you have to be careful what you say to workers these days; doesn't take much to get their dander up. Boy, things sure have changed since I was a worker. The things people expect these days. Well, it makes my hair stand on end. Only the other day I had a request for time off to take some stupid examination. That Jennings guy, he's taking a course in management somewhere. Ha, I guess he's pushing for a promotion. Fat chance he's got while I am around."

Jack: "Fact is, Jim, we have a lot of good people on the payroll, employees who have proved themselves in the past, and we have a lot more with good potential. They just don't seem to put out."

Jim: "I know, I know, you're absolutely right. We just have to motivate them more; they just don't seem to care about work any more. Down right lazy, they are. You just gotta check and control 'em more and more, I say. They make all kinds of excuses, but I don't listen. One guy had the nerve to tell me last week that he had some good ideas on how to improve things in my department. I sorted him out real quick. 'I don't want your goddam ideas,' I said, 'I want results.' That shut him up. Real fast."

Jack: "Good for you, Jim. Give them an inch, and they'll take a mile. You know what bugs me? All these damn meetings we keep having. They drive me crazy. I don't know where it is all going to end. On top of that, I have people lined up outside my door asking me what to do next, and how to do this, and how to do that. I need help, that's what I need."

Jim: I sure know what you mean, Jack. I have workers bringing their problems all the time. So many people seem to depend on me for solutions. Hell, we both need help. More staff, that's what we need, or at least an assistant manager apiece, eh?" (He leans forward and looks eagerly at Jack for confirmation.)

Jack: "You betcha, it's like I always said, if you work like a horse — they let you; they aren't going to stop you killing yourself. No way. You know, I don't mind working long hours — put in 60 last week — if only I could get out from under. From now on, Jim, I'm telling you, I'm going to tighten up around my department, and I'm going to demand efficiency. Yes sir, and I mean EFFICIENCY." (He bangs his glass on the table to emphasize his point.) "Work harder and be more efficient, that's what I'm going to tell 'em at the meeting next week. And boy, am I going to lay it on."

Jim: "It's the only way to go, man. It's the only way to go. Let's drink to that." (They both raise their glasses in triumph.)

EXERCISE:

You happen to overhear this conversation in a bar one night.

How would you diagnose the corporate condition in which Jim and Jack are working?

Do Jim and Jack remind you of anyone you know?

If so, who? Try to be honest.

Would you want to work for Jim or Jack?

Why not?

Identify three things they should stop doing,

and three things they sould start doing to reduce their problems.

Would you dare to let your staff discuss this dialogue between Jim and Jack at one of your staff meetings?

If not, why not? Try to be honest.

CHAPTER XVII

The Wisdom Of Women

A good example of how women are humiliated, intimidated, and 'shrunk' in the world of work is graphically portrayed in the smash movie, *Nine To Five*, starring Dolly Parton, Jane Fonda, and Lily Tomlin. Despite some exaggeration and a strong comedic element,the underlying theme of the film is a bitter protest against the treatment of women at work. My own experience in a number of corporate dramas only confirms the attitude and behavior of many Bosses toward women. How women feel about their Bosses was strikingly revealed in the film during the acting out of fantasies of revenge by several female employees. Beneath the hilarious context of these fantasies, in which several women employees showed how they would like to treat their Bosses if roles could be reversed,is a stark documentation of how corporate dinosaurs create a breeding ground for pygmies in the world of work. In *Nine To Five* the pygmies eventually revolt, and, during the absence of the hated Boss, show what can be achieved. When the Boss returns he is astounded and humiliated to be informed by the chairman of the board that his department has achieved a 30% increase in productivity during his absence. What the female pygmies managed to achieve, which was considered so remarkable, is happening in many corporations as a matter of course under Leaders. Leaders are anxious to give women as much Vitamin O (Opportunity) as they can handle, and there are plenty of women around in the world of work who are more than willing to prove what they can achieve. Some outstanding examples of successful women in Canada are Madame Jean Sauve, as first woman speaker in the House of Commons. Flora MacDonald, former Minister of external affairs. Jean Wadds, as Canada's High Commissioner in London. Shirley Carr, vice-president of the 2.3 million member Canadian Labour Congress, and one of the most powerful female labour leaders in the Western world. And, of course, many women are now begining to ascend executive and managerial heights for the very first time in a number of corporations. However, Statistics Canada shows that 62% of women are concentrated in jobs conventionally held by women. Only 2.7% hold positions in management, and about 1% serve on boards of directors.

The Women's Bureau of the Federal Department of Labour has revealed that the average wage of the full-time working woman in 1977 was $9,143 compared to $15,818 for men. Any thinking person must question why women have for so long been unjustly diminished in the world of work, and deprived of equal wages. The answer, of course, lies in the historical treatment of women down through the ages when, for the most part, they were treated as chattels, inferiors, and in my sense of the word, pygmies. In spite of the vast contribution made by women in two world wars, many Bosses in many corporations still keep women down and fail to give them the opportunity to make any creative contribution.

Banks have been notorious in this regard. It took the threat of unionization to improve working conditions in a few of the major banks, but complaints about Bosses are rife among female employees. Some female employees have been dismissed for getting involved in union activities. Many still complain bitterly regarding the lack of respect and dignity afforded them at work. With bank profits soaring, it is hard to understand why women employees cannot be paid equal wages for equal work.

During a librarians strike in the City of Toronto in 1980, a number of female librarians complained that they too were denied respect and dignity at their place of work. Authoritarian systems are an affront to women of intelligence, regardless of their calling. Certain hospitals have created more problems for themselves by maintaining a rigid Boss-subordinate system, than by anything else. There are many supervisors in hospitals who are highly proficient technically, but woefully deficient in their ability to deal with employees. Most of these supervisors are women. They are just as capable as being Bosses as men. They have been denied Vitamin O, in terms of opportunities to learn about modern management. I remember working with the director of nursing of a large hospital, who was superbly qualified in nursing, and who worked six and sometimes seven days a week. The nurses revolted and threatened to strike. Why? They were being Bossed to death, checked, controlled, supervised, but never listened to. They had lots of ideas on how to improve efficiency and effectiveness, but their Boss would not listen. I told this lady Boss that a very good definition of a manager is someone who can stay dead in their office for a long time without anyone knowing. She was horrified. I had to explain to her that if you have people constantly running to you with all of their little problems, as she did, you are well on the way to creating pygmies.

I am happy to be able to say that this particular Boss listened and learned.

I am constantly reading the good advice that is being handed out to women who want to break into management in the world of work. "Go to business school and graduate in business administration" is a constant theme. Unfortunately, the numbers-oriented courses at graduate schools of business minimize the area in which women excel: intuition and creativity. Business schools teach managers to play it safe. Innovation and creativity, despite all the lip service, is largely ignored. With all the stress on sophisticated tools of management, they seldom, if ever, address themselves to the basic art of management, which lies in how to create an environment in which persons, not pygmies, become self-motivated. There is a lot of talk about motivation. Oh yes, but little realization that no one can motivate anyone else, because people are always highly motivated in terms of doing things *they want to do*. Women are experts in motivation. They know how to listen and they are more sensitive to the emotional nuances that affect the decision making process.

Ashley Montagu, in his book *The Natural Superiority of Women*, states categorically that women are "physically, psychologically, and socially superior to men." He points out that they live, on an average, five to six years longer, and they are more stable emotionally.

There is no doubt that women have already proved that they can do many nontraditional jobs as well as, if not better, than men.

In the historic, patriarchal systems of management which have prevailed for centuries, obedience to authority was the main virtue in the established hierarchies. However, in a matriarchal order, all men are perceived as equal, since they are all born of mothers. The fundamental bond in a matriarchal order is the equality of all men and respect for human life. These values have for too long been absent in our patriarchal systems of management which urgently need an infusion of female insight into the critical areas of quality of work life issues in the 1980s.

CHAPTER XVIII

The Management Paradox

Most management has little management in it: a steadily increasing proportion of the student's time is devoted to technical subjects.

Business Horizons

Professor L. Sayles of Columbia University reports that there is a strange paradox in the field of management education today. In the midst of an upsurge of interest in business administration, the actual study of management is declining. (see *Contemporary Readings in Organizational Behavior*, 1977.)

Professor Sayles states that the reliance on case studies in management training is not adequate, and neither is the training in human relations and communications. He deplores the extreme emphasis on quantitative methods, and he suggests that this is caused by those who feel the need for academic respectability.

Developing a beautiful mathematical model

does not necessarily mean that it bears any resemblance to reality in the world of work. It was Einstein who said, "As far as the laws of mathematics refer to reality, they are not certain, and as far as they are certain, they do not refer to reality." Certain kinds of Bosses are very impressed with the abstractions of management, and they like to have employees who are graduates from schools of management abstraction. Results-oriented Leaders in a number of corporations are cautious about hiring hot-shot abstractors who have difficulty in translating management abstractions into concrete results. As Peter Drucker has pointed out many times: "Employers, and especially large companies need to look in their workforce for the people of proven performance and willingness to achieve, though they lack the formal qualifications." (*The Age of Discontinuity*, p. 332.)

How many times have you read an advertisement in the help wanted columns that said: "We are more interested in your ability to get results than in your qualifications on paper." Not very often. Why? Because more Bosses are advertising than Leaders.

Daniel Yankelovich, in *The Worker and the Job* (p. 19), makes the following observation: "The cult of efficiency may well be breeding inefficiency. It is quite possible that the gains in productivity achieved annually by technology, by the infusion of capital, and by formal methods of management and organization are more than offset by the tendency to create conditions in the name of efficiency that make it impossible for people to feel they are doing a good job or that what they do on the job counts."

This is a well-stated warning to Bosses that

their haste to install the latest technology may well be counter productive, if they overlook the human side of management. Bosses will reply to this by saying that with robots making robots, and silicon chips, who cares? We won't need people anymore. I am all for any technology that liberates pygmies and eliminates meaningless work, and if that means fewer people in the world of work, what's wrong with that? Do we live to work, or do we work to live? It has been said that North Americans don't know much about the art of living. They don't have enough time, because they are too busy working. Let's not forget that we have moved into the post-industrial era and a leisure-oriented economy and culture. In the meantime, it is the responsibility of politicians, who are leaders by definition, to think about the effective deployment, re-training, and upgrading of people caught up in any technological revolution. They had better come up with something better than unemployment insurance, or they will have a lot of very unhappy people on top of them. I believe that every politician should be required by law to attend courses in management and leadership conducted by people with practical and successful experience. A politician's mandate is to assist in managing the country and the economy.

CHAPTER XIX

Dinosaur Detector Quiz

	True	False
1) A good working environment is required to provide real job satisfaction.	☐	☐
2) Money is the most important motivator.	☐	☐
3) A good definition of management is planning, organizing, and controlling.	☐	☐
4) The main features of MBO is an emphasis on techniques in setting objectives.	☐	☐
5) Higher level needs are more important than lower level needs.	☐	☐

6) A standard of performance measures the person doing the job.
☐ ☐

7) Quality of Work Life relates to improving the environment in which work is done.
☐ ☐

8) Sociotechnical analysis is a sociological analysis of an organization.
☐ ☐

9) Motivating people is a major part of a manager's job.
☐ ☐

10) Training and developing people are basically one and the same thing.
☐ ☐

11) Your employees should accept you as their natural leader.
☐ ☐

12) Employees always appreciate an improvement in working conditions.
☐ ☐

If you marked each item as FALSE, you got each one right. Chances are good that you are a Leader and a people stretcher. If you marked most items as TRUE, chances are good that you are a Boss, and without knowing it you are producing pygmies.

CHAPTER XX

Utopia
Nowhere Or Now Here

If you believe that prevention is better than cure, you will probably agree that preventing strikes is better than constantly battling to resolve them.

In 1978, DeHavilland Aircraft Co. lost nearly $60 million during a fifteen week strike. In 1976, Alcan lost $90 million through a five and a half month strike. The Abitibi Paper Co. lost $8.2 million some time ago, and so it goes, on and on, a dismal tale of losses for management, employees, and communities across the land.

Canada has the world's worst record for strikes, and each year absenteeism costs the country more than $4 billion dollars, or 3½ times what the Unemployment Insurance Commission pays out in one year. Something in the order of 500,000 workers fail to turn up each day through illness and injury, or because they don't feel like it, and close to 125 million man-days of work are lost each year.

Most Bosses, including union Bosses, scorn the idea that improved management could improve the situation. They regard such ideas as Utopian. The word Utopia means Nowhere, or Now here. Bosses fail to recognize, or are unwilling to admit, that the solutions to many of the problems afflicting business and industry are NOW HERE. They have been applied successfully, or are in the process of being applied by Leaders here in Canada and the United States and in many countries around the world. For example: At Windsor, Ontario, Shell Oil has built the first oil refinery in the world on a NOW HERE revolutionary QWL, or Quality of Work Life approach to prevention rather than cure.

Bell Canada, Northern Electric, Philips, Steinbergs, Miracle Mart, Alcan, General Foods & Proctor & Gamble have all reported successes in the application of QWL principles.

The endless search for ways to improve economic performance has produced an astounding proliferation of management menus offering an incredible range of esoteric fare, all designed to 'motivate' employees to do dull work with enthusiasm. Unfortunately, this vast outpouring of psychedelic snake oil has not succeeded in curing the innumerable strikes and other assorted ailments that afflict the corporate body.

Einstein used to say that "imagination is more important than knowledge." While there seems to be no lack of imagination in grinding out gimmicks for the marketplace, there is a real lack of imagination on the part of Bosses in empathizing with their employees. It is lack of imagination that accounts for the neglect of a company's greatest asset: the desire of its people to be involved in the achievement of challenging goals. The greatest poverty is not in dollars, it is in lack of imagination in harnessing human resources, and preventing people from being converted into pygmies.

The majority of corporations are either not aware or not interested in what is happening. They are not AWAKE. Corporations like Shell, Manufacturers Life Insurance, MacMillan Bloedel, Petrosar Ltd., Supreme Aluminum, and B.C. Forest Products, are exercising real Leadersip in redesigning jobs to make them more interesting and challenging, and giving employees more freedom and responsibility.

At the new refinery run by Shell at Sarnia, groups of workers carry out an entire operation from start to finish. More than that, they decide how and when they will carry out work procedures. The aura of the Boss has been diminished by the elimination of supervisors, time clocks, and other 19th century memorabilia. Worried about the unions co-operating? Neil Reimer, who is the director of the Oil, Chemical and Atomic Workers, says that his union was formed "to improve the quality of life of our members. When companies come to realize that they can get more and better work from an employee by humanizing his job and giving him a say in how it's designed and performed, then it is our duty as a union to co-operate in making that desired change."

The team concept of working has replaced the traditional method at Manufacturers Life. Again, groups of workers drawn from different specialties take care of the entire process of customer service. Each employee in the team is trained to handle several other jobs so that he or she can interchange at any time.

These revolutionary developments are not Utopian; they are here now, and they are here to stay because Leaders who are awake recognize that prevention is better than cure.

Why is it that most people will work harder away from their work than when they are at work? The greatest vanishing trick in the world is performed at the begining of every working day, when thousands of workers disappear into a job description. From people into pygmies the moment they enter the door to work.

Bosses protest that there are too many jobs around that do not lend themselves to improvment. Leaders know that no job is too small to grow in, if the climate is right.

QWL, or Quality of Work Life, is emerging as the most advanced and all-encompassing program to prevent people from being converted into pygmies in the world of work.

In 1979 I had the opportunity to participate in an intensive, two week, hands-on QWL conference conducted by Professor Lou Davis of the Institute of Industrial Relations, UCLA, Los Angeles. Davis is one of the world's foremost practitioners of QWL, and I was fortunate enough to do some field work under his immediate guidance. Representatives from government and industry were present, I am happy to say, and the general concensus at the end of the program was positive and encouraging.

Quality of Work Life centers are springing up across the country, and universities are now offering courses in the subject on an extension basis. The Federal Government has set up a permanent QWL unit in Ottawa, which issues a regular journal on QWL. It summarizes research, applications, conferences, and other events of related interest across Canada.

QWL as a concept is still growing and is hard to pin down in a concise definition, but Ted Mills of the American Center for the Quality of Working Life puts it this way: "Quality of Work Life is not a system but a process — based on human interaction at work. It's a way of working suggesting that working people can be provided the opportunity to seek — together — to identify barriers to the effectiveness of their work organization, or their part of it, and through problem solving, tumble those barriers down, one by one."

Einar Thorsrud, head of the Work Research Institute, Oslo, and recognized as an expert in QWL, defines the concept as follows:

> QWL is not a new discipline or subject, like economics, psychology, sociology, industrial engineering, etc. It builds on these and related disciplines and is characterised by an inter-disciplinary approach to problems of working life. It also observes the interdependence between work and the quality of life in general. Therefore, family and community life is part of the wide problem area covered by QWL, the centre of which is the organization of work.

Quite obviously, QWL is a wide ranging concept, and it's implications in terms of physical, mental, and social well being are staggering. If every organization in North America adopted QWL as a way of managing its human and physical resources, there would be no more pygmies in the world of work. Let's take a look at some of the specific factors in the work place that QWL seeks to ensure:

1) Fair pay & benefits
2) Safe Environment
3) Job security
4) Full participation
5) Growth on job
6) Social integration
7) Free bargaining
8) Challenging work
9) Attractive work space

If everything in this list could be taken care of to the satisfaction of all concerned — management, employees, unions, and communities — you can see that just about all of the problems in the world of work would disappear. Of course, that is unlikely to happen in the near future. But don't laugh, we're moving in that direction!

At the federal level, there is already in place a Joint Committee on Quality of Work Life, manned by the Secretary of the Treasury Board, the Chairman of the Public Service Commisssion, the Deputy Minister of Labour Canada, and the Presidents of the various Public Service Unions participating in a variety of Quality of Work Life initiatives. Eric Trist, a renowned leader in QWL from the Tavistock Institute in Enland, is now working for the Federal Government as strategic Consultant. So you see, there are some very big guns aimed at eliminating pygmies from the work place in Canada. It is probably the best thing that has happened in Canada, so far as industrial relations is concerned, in the last one hundred years.

Trial projects in QWL have been conducted in the Dept. of Taxation in London, Ontario, Statistics Canada, and the State Department in Ottawa. At Statistics Canada, 30 keypunch operators were permitted to hire a consultant to assist them in their efforts to design a more productive work enviroment. They invited proposals from several consultants and set up a task force to look into ways of controlling their own work. These pilot projects are the spearhead of what will undoubtedly become a major thrust in developing ways to improve productivity and morale.

The QWL approach to liberating pygmies in the world of work, and improving profit at the same time, is preceded by what is known as a socio-technical analysis of organizational structure. The rationale here is that every organization comprises a technical system and a social system, and that each system must be analysed to identify and remove blocks, and then integrated to optimize the productivity of both.

This socio-technical method is a 'bottom up' type of redesign and change, in contrast to job enrichment or work improvement, which is often 'top down' in process.

Working in autonomous or semi-autonomous groups, employees are freed from external controls and learn to develop internal controls. In effect, they learn to manage themselves. They start moving from parent-child to adult-to-adult relationships with management. From pygmies to people.

Keep in mind that QWL is predicated on the assumption that successful implementation of its procedures will optimize the production of profit by optimizing the production of human and physical resources. I don't want you to get the idea that QWL is some kind pseudo-intellectual crusade for bleeding hearts and do-gooders. It is a highly disciplined and hard-headed approach to satisfying the needs of both management and labor.

Under QWL, employees start to work because they feel an obligation to conform to the group norms, which *they* have helped to develop. In other words, because "the need to belong" is very strong, employees become self-motivated from within, rather than just motivated by orders and money. When a group of employees starts to develop a work culture of its own, it creates a climate which inhibits behavior that will adversely affect the interests of the group.

What QWL is trying to bring about in our world of work is very similar to what the Japanese have already succeeded in doing in their world of work. If they have not been applying QWL as a way of life in the workplace as we understand it, they have certainly applied JWL — Japanese Way of Life — with resounding success. Why are we so far behind?

East and West are indeed moving closer to each other, by virtue of some common denominator of human experience that as yet, eludes our cortical connections. Remember Zen: "Don't think, LOOK." LOOK OUT! Corporate Dinosaurs, LOOK OUT! Bosses, this is not UTOPIA. This is not nowhere, This is NOW HERE.

CHAPTER XXI

N/aCH + O = R

Dr. David McLelland of Harvard University has spent a lifetime trying to discover why only a small minority of people seem to have a natural drive to work hard in pursuit of personal goals. Over the years he has undertaken a vast amount of research in a number of countries around the world, all of which is fully documented and summarized in his magnum opus, *The Achieving Society.*

McLelland has identified a distinct motive which he claims can be found and tested in any group of people. He calls this motive, the Need For Achievement, or, N/aCH. Persons with this need, claims McLelland, spend a great deal of time thinking up ways of improving their performance in whatever they do.

He suggests that N/aCH people are not born with a need for achievement, but they develop the need in response to warm, nonautocratic parents who encourage them to set demanding but achievable goals.

When people think a great deal in terms of

125

their need for achievement, things begin to happen. McLelland has established that this is true, not only for individuals, but for nations as well. When nations constantly search for ways of improving their performance, they actually do. The histories of ancient Greece, Spain, England, and other nations, regardless of left or right political orientation, all bear testimony to McLelland's astounding findings.

The question is whether the need for achievement can be developed and applied to further economic progress, wherever desired.

Over the years David McLelland has conducted a number of courses for business men in different parts of the world to explain the significance of N/aCH and the importance of setting carefully planned goals over a period of time, usually two years. In every case but one, he was able to demonstrate statistically that the men who completed his special training had done better than comparable men who had either had not taken his training, or who had taken some other kind of management course.

McLelland points out in his book that it took him twenty years and hundreds of thousands of dollars to develop his findings, but he is still having a difficult time persuading Bosses that he is on to something worth looking into. "There is no real substitute for ideological fervour," he writes, "a country or at least a significant portion of its elite has got to want economic achievement badly enough to give it priority over other desires." Think of Japan! It lost in war, but it is winning in peace. And how! In general terms, the need for achievement is apparent in large numbers of employees that most Bosses would describe as either indif-

ferent or lazy in performing their work. Ever
noticed how often people will tell you they hate
work. But, oh boy, do they ever love ACHIEVE-
MENT. Why? Because work seldom provides opportunities for people to show what they can do.

Here's what I mean. Think of the scads of people you know who volunteer their services to
countless clubs, churches, and agencies. Same deal
in every village, town, and city across North
America. So what? Well, these people may not give
a damn about how their company is doing, but they
will be greatly concerned about how well their
favorite charity, school drive, or church benefit is
doing. And well you know it. In these kinds of
situations, people, ordinary everyday people, will
work infinitely harder for nothing than they ever
will for money. Why? Because they feel needed,
they feel important, they get recognition, and they
love ACHIEVEMENT.

The abiding tragedy of 'Corporate Pygmies
Unlimited' is that they are trapped in situations
where the only challenge comes in outwitting or
sabotaging the system and frustrating the hell out
of the Boss.

Funny thing, though, in a crisis these meta-
phorical pygmies can turn into giants. As Peter
Drucker has so often reminded us, ordinary people
can do extraordinary things, under the right conditions.

Magnificent achievements are possible in
peace and in war, if those invisible assets of human
energy are liberated. Leaders know this and they
know well how to rub the genie's lamp and bring
forth a brilliant flow of talent and effort in achieve-
ing personal and corporate goals. That's why they
lead the field.

Time and again I meet workers in different organizations who show me how they could improve their methods of working "if only we were allowed to." Not too long ago, I visited a group of men on the night shift at a well known plant in Hamilton. They showed me a new tooling device they had invented which greatly improved results. Sadly, they told me, they could only use it during the night shift because the daytime Boss would not allow it. They had to fudge their production sheets to account for the nightly increase in productivity.

What does it all add up to? Let's tune in and listen to McLelland for a moment: "Pay attention to the effects that your plans will have on values, motives, and attitudes of people because *in the long run* it is these factors that will determine whether plans are successful in speeding economic development." (*The Achieving Society*, p. 393.)

To Bosses, all of this is some kind of unbelievable mystery. To Leaders, however, it is all expressed in a very simple formula:

$$N/aCH + O = R$$

THE NEED FOR ACHIEVEMENT, PLUS OPPORTUNITY, EQUALS RESULTS.

Please don't take my word for it. Try it. It works.

CHAPTER XXII

The Perfect Employee?

Micromania is the latest affliction affecting the nervous systems of corporations. Cortical mosaics throughout the land are throbbing with a terrible intensity in response to the thrills and chills of electronic hopes and fears.

Microelectronics threatens to transform work or eliminate it altogether. In some parts of Europe the alarm bells are ringing loud and clear. Predictions in West Germany estimate that up to 40% of all office work will be eliminated, and in France, estimates indicate that more than 30% of bank and insurance personnel are likely to lose their jobs in the not too distant future.

It is estimated that unemployment in Britain will increase by up to 25% in the next decade as a result of the micro-chip. According to a report in 1980 by the Science Council of Canada, things may develop a little more slowly in Canada because the implications of the new technology are still being assessed. However, the Montreal Institute for Research on Public Policy has predicted coldly and boldly that one million women will be out of work by 1990 due to the impact of microelectronics.

To what extent will operators become subservient to these new micro-marvels? Will micromania prove to be counterproductive in terms of human motivation? There is a real danger that if this new technology is not installed and operated with a view to enriching jobs, rather than diminishing them in terms of opportunity and achievement, employees — 90% of whom are women — will be downgraded to pygmy status in the world of work.

This would be a great step backward for women who have fought hard to gain improved status and opportunity for advancement in the workplace. Women need this like they need a hole in the head. One school of thought argues that low-skilled jobs will disappear and will be replaced by more complex jobs requiring a much better education.

The fact is, whichever way you slice it, the reduction of challenge, the loss of opportunity, and the dangers of depersonalization, could create serious repercussions that would adversely affect the economy.

Corporate Leaders who give serious thought to installing these new technological triumphs will make sure they do not create a 20th century version of a 19th century assembly line operation.

As things look now, a fortunate few can expect to be upgraded from typists to word processors, and in this process they will undoubtedly find both opportunity and challenge. As for the others, most of the others, a big question mark remains.

In the final analysis, it is people, not pygmies, who make any new technology work effectively. If

Bosses impose it on people without due consideration of their needs, it may turn out to be just one more internal problem that will accelerate the demise of the corporate dinosaur.

CHAPTER XXIII

Up Your Corporate Dinosaur

According to Dr. R. Swinton of the Royal Ontario Museum, the dinosaurs of prehistoric times depended on a particular form of plant life to provide them with a laxative. It is believed that the plant in question was a fern that ceased to grow, and thereby deprived the dinosaurs of a vital element in their diet. According to this theory, the dinosaurs died of congested bowels. An ignominious demise, to say the least. Whether or not the plight of the original dinosaurs is relevant to the plight of corporate dinosaurs today, is something the reader must judge for himself. It does seem apparent, however, that many corporate dinosaurs — as I have defined them — are suffering from severe internal disorders.

A corporation is, by definition, a system that requires inputs to be converted into outputs. If, deep in the inner workings of a corporate body, too many pygmies accumulate and get bogged down in the process of converting inputs into outputs, the result will be a serious decline in quality and quantity of work. When this situation occurs, it is one of the major symptoms of an unhealthy corporate body, and if it is allowed to continue without treatment, it can convert a healthy corporation into a corporate dinosaur, and a member of an endangered species.

It was Santayana who once said: "Those who cannot remember the past are condemned to repeat it." We might do well to ponder the past in considering the corporate dinosaurs of today. Cortical complacency is a major factor in the sluggish movement and growth of the corporate dinosaur. To improve the output of any system, the inputs must be fully developed and co-ordinated, and the activities of people must be geared to specific results. People input in terms of energy, imagination, experience, and enthusiasm, are of vital importance.

Unless people are fully involved at all levels, the corporate body will not be able to deliver the goods. The more it tries to get things under control, the more things get out of control. Constriction of the cortical function is a very real problem for every corporate body by virtue of its traditional pyramidal structure. Although there are signs that some corporate pyramids are widening at the top, the majority maintain a rigid and increasingly brittle stance. Under these conditions, complacency will increasingly corrode the cortical connections, and diminish the spark and muscle tone of the corporate body, and people will be converted into pygmies by the bucketful. The only cure for cortical constriction — and by this I mean the limitations of the combined neural networks of all managerial and supervisory staff — is to ensure a three-way flow of Vitamin I up, down, and across the corporate body. Without Vitamin I, or Information, people become pygmies because they become dependent on Bosses. Every corporate dinosaur is subjected to severe internal pressure from its pygmies, who persist in doing only what they are told to do. If there happens to be nothing to do, they will wait to be told what to do next. Very often, under these circumstances, the corporate dinosaur finds that it has to employ more and more pygmies who will actually wind up doing less and less. The Law of Diminishing Returns sets in with a vengeance. The source of the 'human energy crisis' in the world of work lies concealed inside every corporate dinosaur. The waste is tragic, to say nothing of the resulting boredom, absenteeism, and poor productivity. The solution is to treat people like adults, and encourage them to stretch and grow. You don't believe me? Ask the Japanese.

Corporate dinosaurs of all species are highly centralized in their functions. Everything is arranged from top down, and people become personnel, or, in my language, pygmies. Most decisions are made at the top, and then passed down to the pygmies at lower levels. They are told what to do, and in most cases, how to do it. This is the traditional pattern of management, whether it be in G.M., the Federal Government, the local grocery store, a hospital, or a university. Keep in mind that this model of management was designed originally to discipline armies. It is no longer relevant to corporate life in the 20th century. Like human bodies, corporate bodies go through various stages of growth from childhood to the infirmities of old age. Unlike people, however, the corporate body can keep going for hundreds of years, if properly managed. Of course, not every corporate body is destined to become a dinosaurial disaster. A period of stagnation in corporate growth and performance need not ring the death knell, if caught in time. While resurrection from rigor mortis is unlikely, rejuvenation from stagnation is possible.

In prescribing a cure for corporate constriction, it is essential to ensure a healthy flow of self-motivated people. This will not only help to prevent a hardening of the corporate arteries, it will help to prevent an equally serious disorder known as a hardening of the corporate categories. Next, a top-down move from win-lose adversarial relationships to win-win co-operative relationships with unions is essential. It can be done, and it is being done in numerous corporate bodies across North America.

Corporate survival depends on Leaders who are future focussed. They make the future happen; they are pro-active, not reactive, and they know what business they are in. Do you? What business would you say Xerox is in? Duplication? Wrong. Education is the largest part of their business. What business do you think IBM is in. Computers? Wrong. They sell solutions to problems. What business would you say Bell Telephone is in? Telephones? Wrong. Bell Telephone is no longer Bell Telephone, it is Bell Canada, and its business is the electronic communication of information. What business would you say the passenger shipping lines are in? Transportation? Wrong. They are in the hotel business. Think about it. What business are you in, and what business will you be in five years from now? If you don't know, you may be out of business. You are not looking ahead. You are not future focussed.

Internal communications are vital for survival. Every corporate body requires built-in, anti-self deception devices in the shape of feed-back systems to facilitate bottom-up communication. External communications require a corporate capacity to evolve and revolve psychic antennae to pick up clues, and cues on what is going on 'out there'. One Boss of a fair sized corporation was in trouble with his community neighbors because fallout from his stacks polluted all the local laundry hanging out to dry. "I don't care about what is going on 'out there' he said, "I care only about what is going on in this company." He didn't last long. He couldn't 'see' and he couldn't 'hear'.

Cortical catharsis is good for the corporate psyche, and helps to burn the carbon off the cortical carburretor. This can be done by bottom-up meetings with representatives from all levels to look at the good and bad things that have happened over the previous year. This is the time for smart Leaders to find out what they can do to help their people do a better job. To clean out the cortical connections at corporate H.Q. may require a Retreat For Cortical Clones, plus a couple of good indigenous sparkplugs, plus a tip-top catalytic consultant.

Removal of corporate cataracts is essential to remove psychological blindness. What corporate dinosaurs look at is not what they see; it is what they believe. If corporate dinosaurs could 'see' their problems, they could solve them, because the best consultants they could ever hire are already on their payroll.

Full delegation of the cerebral functions throughout the corporate anatomy is mandatory so that people closest to the action will have real decision-making power. People thinking and working like PEOPLE is the best possible way to prevent corporate decay.

In addition to the above, corporate rejuvenation requires the addition of psycho-vitamins to the daily diet of people at all levels of the corporate body. Remember, Vitamin A for Achievement, Vitamin R for Responsibility, Vitamin O for Opportunity, Vitamin I for Information, and Vitamin R2 for Recognition. Without these essential vitamins your people will succumb to the sickness known as SICKNESS OF THE JOB. And finally, every employee should have a clear vision of corporate goals and objectives. People cannot achieve what they cannot define.

Remember the bricklayers? One said "I am building a wall. The other said: "I am building a cathedral."

What are your employees building for you?

If they are pygmies, they are building a wall, and building you OUT.

If they are people, they are building a cathedral, and building you IN.

In conclusion, let me remind you that the dinosaur in your driveway is running out of time and energy. Thoughtful people are switching over to new, more efficient, and more effective models. The corporate dinosaur you work for is also running out of time and energy. Human Energy. Thoughtful Leaders are switching over to new, more efficient, and more effective organizational models.

How about you?

CHAPTER XXIV

QWL And Preparing For Change: What To Do, And How To Start Doing It

The most advanced overall strategy for improving performance and productivity in the western world of work undoubtedly lies in the QWL (Quality of Work Life) ideas and methods mentioned earlier in this book. The QWL approach is essentially long term and cannot be put into effect overnight. In addition, it requires the whole-hearted support of all levels of management and union. If you are interested in learning more about QWL procedures you can start by reading the literature on the subject. Two definitive and substantial books are available, edited by Professor Lou Davis and Dr. Albert Cherns. *The Quality of Working Life* is in two volumes (paperback), published by Free Press. They are well worth reading and will provide you with an excellent orientation to the new horizons that are opening up in the world of work.

A number of Universities in Canada and in the United States offer one and two day workshops on QWL practices and procedures which are usually very informative and helpful because of the questions raised and the opinions expressed. Labour Canada and certain provinces — notably Ontario — offer access to numerous reports and studies in the field of QWL. Ontario has an excellent Quality of Work Life Centre manned by Dr. Hans van Beinum, an expert from Holland. In approaching the subject of QWL it would be wise to keep in mind the words of Roy F. Bennet, a president of Ford Motor Company:

> Employee involvement is not a short term programme. . . . Employee involvement very definitely necessitates a change in management style. The employee involvement programme is a change from the authoritarian [Boss] style of management to one of a participatory [Leader] nature, where there is an opportunity for an upward as well as downward communication within the organization.

Perspectives on QWL

QWL is based on humanistic values, and incorporates democratic principles into its functions. QWL is not a substitute for collective bargaining, nor does it seek to remove a realistic relationship at the bargaining table. It creates a new area for consultation between labor and management on matters that do not lend themselves to arbitration.

QWL is no cut and dried formula approach to solving organizational problems. Each organization must develop a tailor made design to suit its own peculiar needs. A certain sequence of steps is usually followed:

Step 1 A discussion and review of QWL concepts is initiated by either management or the union. Representatives of both sides will get together at a later date to establish whether a mutual desire exists to move away from traditional win-lose to win-win relationships.

Step 2 If QWL is considered worth trying, a third party will be brought in to provide a complete orientation to its ideas and methods.

Step 3 Agreement is reached between company and union regarding objectives, terms of reference, and plans.

Step 4 A steering committee is set up to oversee the QWL project or projects, and to determine their location. The selected site will often be in an area where productivity is low.

Step 5 The Steering Committee prepares to implement the project, and to this end it must obtain the support of the manager in charge of the area selected for the project.

Step 6 Project teams are formed. These are composed of workers elected by their peers in the actual project site area. This will be preceded by a joint management-union announcement to explain the procedures.

Step 7 The project team commences to analyse individual jobs and the general working environment.

Step 8 Recommendations for change are prepared, based on data collected by project team or teams.

Step 9 Evaluation to determine if the project or projects have achieved their objectives.

(For an excellent and detailed outline of these steps see, *Quality of Work Life Ideas and Methods*, a booklet published by Labour Canada in September 1978.)

It cannot be emphasized too strongly that the QWL approach is one that cannot be undertaken by any organization until everyone involved is throughly conversant with its ideology and methods. All concerned must be fully committed to the practice of QWL over the long haul.

For those organizations that are not yet ready for a full scale commitment to QWL, there are a number of ways in which individual managers can prepare for positive change. If you are interested in considering some of these ways, you might like to mull over the following questions:

1) Do you allow and encourage your employees to chair staff meetings when you are present?

2) Do you ask your employees for their ideas and opinions on policy issues for which you are responsible?

3) Do you ever allow your employees to represent you at meetings you cannot attend?

4) Do you ever send a memo saying, "Thanks" or "Good work" to a deserving employee?

5) Do you ever invite an employee to read a book on management that has impressed you, and ask for his opinion?

6) Do you ever ask your employees to review *your* job description and objectives?

7) Do you ever alert one of your best workers to an opportunity for promotion within your organization and encourage him, or her, to apply?

8) Do you ever make it possible for at least some of your employees to gain exposure to top management?

9) Have you ever invited union representatives to attend a management seminar?

10) Would you be prepared to assign one of your employees to do research on an important project?

11) Would you allow one of your employees to recruit a new employee on your behalf?

12) Do you invite or order an employee to attend a training course?

13) Do you discuss carefully with employees why

you feel they should attend a training program, and do you explain to them that on completion of their training you will want to hear from them in what way they will apply what they have learned?

14) Do you ever recommend any of your employees to represent your organization on a community project?

15) Do you encourage employees to write you a career and personal development letter each year outlining their plans and achievements?

16) Do you send a management letter to each of your employees each year outlining your objectives and plans, and invite them to reply in writing with their comments and suggestions?

17) Do you invite your employees on a rotating basis to review and summarize management articles and reports for discussion at staff development meetings?

18) Do you keep books on management and technical topics circulating among your staff for regular monthly discussions with you?

19) Do you know how long you can stay dead in your office without anyone knowing? (I just want to see if you are awake! If people are constantly at your door, read on)

20) Is there a sign on your desk that says: DON'T BRING ME PROBLEMS ... BRING ME SOLUTIONS!

21) Do you ever ask your employees this question: "What can I do to help you do a better job"?

If you answer yes to many or most of these questions, you have probably created a working climate that encourages achievement and productivity. Keep it up.

In the world of work the challenge in the 1980s lies in the fact that managers can no longer depend upon their authority to 'motivate' people. Employees are demanding not merely improvement in economic benefits, but also the satisfaction of their needs for personal dignity, recognition, and achievement.

Examine carefully the daily diet of work you give to your employees. Does it contain those all important psychovitamins discussed earlier in this book? A healthy work diet contributes mightily to self-respect and personal well being. Remember, people feel their best when they are doing their best. Are you doing *your* best to help them do *their* best?

Appendix

RESULTS OF EMPLOYEE INVOLVEMENT IN CORPORATE BODIES

CN — clerical employees reorganized work, and by 1970 absenteeism and turnover declined from $66.7 million — up to $23 milion, 52.6% from 1970.

ALCAN — work reorganized so that 1,600 employees managed their own time. Production increased and turnovers decreased.

BELL CANADA, Montreal — Phone installers saved an average of 30 — 60 minutes per day. In one period productivity increased 15%.

CANADIAN LIQUID AIR, Quebec — Workers given increased responsibility and decision making power. They decided to increase working time from 8 hours per day, for 5 days each week — to 12 hours a day for 7 days every 2 weeks. Productivity has increased 10 to 15%

CANADIAN TIRE CORP. — Earnings moved from $81 million to $482 million in 4 years. Average 20-year employee worth $500,000 in shares and benefits.

SUPREME ALUMINUM CO., — Moved from 6th to first place in 4 years. All employees received $3,110 in 1974 as their share of profits. Nearly half of them are shareholders.

Some other corporations in North America that are working on employee involvement programs:

Monsanto Textiles Co.
Alcan Aluminum
Philips Electrical Industries
Oldsmobile Lansing, Michigan
Corning Glass
Donnelly Mirrors, Inc., Michigan
Weyerhauser, Tacoma Washington
Syntex Corp., Mexico City
H.P. Hood & Sons, Boston
AT&T
Polaroid
Kaiser Aluminum
Bankers Trust, New York
C.I.L.
Sears Roebuck
Chase Manhattan Bank
Proctor & Gamble
General Foods
Texas Instruments
Kelloggs
Xerox Corporation
Whirlpool
Kodak

Standard Oil
Simpsons Sears
Simpsons Ltd.
Lincoln Electric
Dominion Foundries
Canada Packers
Northern Electric
Valley City Mfg.
Inco (Sudbury)
Ontario Hydro
Midland Industries
The Group at Cox (Hamilton)
Esso Chemical (Sarnia)
Domtar (Toronto)
Hayes Dana Ltd. (St. Thomas)
Steelcase Canada
Union Carbide Canada
Petrosar (Sarnia)
Shell Oil (Sarnia)
Baycoat Ltd. (Hamilton)
Canadian General Electric

Bibliography

I. BOOKS

Alberta Government. *Human Resource Management: Changing Times in Alberta*. Alberta Labour Report, 1979.

Beckett, John A. *Management Dynamics (The New Synthesis)*. New York: McGraw Hill, 1971.

Dalton, Lawrence & Greiner. *Organizational Change and Development*. Irwin Dorsey, 1970.

Davis, L. E. and Cherns, A. B. *The Quality of Working Life*. Volumes I & II. New York: Free Press, 1975.

Drucker, Peter. *The Age of Discontinuity*. New York: Harper & Row, 1971.

Drucker, Peter. *The Future of Industrial Man*. Signet, 1970.

Drucker, Peter. *Management Tasks and Responsibilities*. New York: Harper & Row, 1973.

Drucker, Peter. *Managing for Results*. New York: Harper & Row, 1964.

Drucker, Peter. *The Practice of Management*. New York: Harper & Row, 1954.

Drucker, Peter. *Technology, Management & Society*. New York: Harper & Row, 1970.

Fuller, Buckminster. *Utopia or Oblivion*. New York: Bantam Books, 1969.

Government of Canada. *Report of the Science Council of Canada, 1978*.

Hayakawa, S. I. *Language in Thought and Action*. New York: Harper & Row, 1949.

Hayakawa, S. I. *Language, Meaning and Maturity*. New York: Harper & Row, 1954.

Homans, George C. *The Human Group*. New York: Harcourt-Brace & World, 1950.

Labour Canada. *Quality of Working Life: The Idea and its Application, 1978*.

Likert, Rensis. *New Patterns of Management*. New York: McGraw-Hill, 1961.

Low, Albert. *Zen and Creative Management*. New York: Anchor Books, 1976.

Luthans, Fred. *Contemporary Readings in Organizational Behaviour*. New York: Prentice-Hall, 1977.

Maslow, A. *Euspychian Management*. Dorsey Press, 1965.

McLelland, David. *The Achieving Society*. New York: D. Van Nostrand Co., 1961.

Ministry of Labour. *An Inventory of Innovative Work Arrangement in Ontario*. Ontario Government, 1978.

Ministry of Labour. *Dealing with Some Obstacles in Innovation in the Workplace*. Ontario Government, 1980.

Ministry of Labour. *Starting Up a Redesign Project*. Ontario Government, 1980.

Montagu, Ashley. *The Natural Superiority of Women*. New York: Collier Books, 1974.

National Center for Productivity and QWL. *Recent Initiatives in Labour Management Cooperation*. Washington, D.C., 1976.

Ordiorne, George. *MBO II: A System of Managerial Leadership for the 80s.* New York: Pearson Pitman, 1979.

Ontario Government. *Report of the Royal Commission on Health and Safety in Mines, 1976.*

Rosow, J. *The Worker and the Job.* New York: Prentice-Hall, 1974.

Townsend, Robert. *Up the Organization.* Fawcett Publications, 1970.

Tarrant, John J. *Drucker.* Boston: Cahners Books Inc., 1976.

Vogel, Ezra. *Japan as No. 1.* New York: Harper Colophon Books, 1979.

Watson, Thomas J. Jr. *A Business and Its Benefits.* New York: McGraw-Hill, 1963.

II. ARTICLES

Drucker, Peter. "Behind Japan's Success." *Harvard Business Review,* January-February, 1981.

Howard, J. "Management Productivity: Rusting Out or Burning Out?" *Western University Business Quarterly,* 1975.

Kets de Vries, Manfred F. R. "Managers Can Drive their Subordinates Mad." *Harvard Business Review.* July-August, 1979.

Levinson, Harry. "Criteria for Choosing Chief Executives." *Harvard Business Review,* July-August, 1980.

McMillan, C. "Japan." *Western University Business Quarterly,* 1980.

Mintzberg, H. "Organization Design: Fashion or Fit." *Harvard Business Review,* January-February, 1981.

Pascale, Richard Tannes. "Zen and the Art of

Management." *Harvard Business Review,* March-April, 1978.

Tavernier, Gerard. "Applying Japanese Techniques in the West." *International Management Journal,* June, 1976.

Brian Spikes studied social psychology and social philosophy at London University. He obtained his diploma in 1949. Since then, he has lived and travelled in many parts of the world. He has worked as a prospector and miner, manpower consultant, and college instructor. For the last ten years he has worked as a free-lance writer and consultant on Human Resources Management. He has conducted leadership development programs for more than ten thousand executives and managers employed by major industrial, business, and government corporations.

He has appeared on numerous radio and television programs from coast-to-coast and overseas, and he is a frequent guest speaker at conferences and conventions. Currently, he is writing his third book, *The Confessions of A Consultant*.